PRED...
PLUTOCRACY

GOVERNMENT COMPUTERS

ADD TO WASTE

by

Anthony J. Windisch, CCP

Aardvark Global Publishing

ISBN 978-1-4276-3342-2

Printed in the United States of America

Fourth Printing

For information or to order additional books, please log on:

www.NumberBrian.com

Dedication

This presentation is dedicated to my mother, Mary Gruendler Windisch, who immigrated from Romania/Hungary to start a new life in our great country. She died in 1996 at the age of ninety. She had to work hard to earn a living for herself and her family. By her example, she inspired me to earn my own way, to always stand for what is right for myself and others, and to never give up.

Special acknowledgement is given to my wife, Dorothy, and my family; federal banking consultant, Frank Spinner; Richard A. Scheitlin, CPA; and my brother, Rev. Adolf M. Windisch, SM, Ph.D.

Contents

Preface

Predatory Plutocracy

Whistleblower Anthony J. Windisch claims our United States government functions similar to a "Predatory Plutocracy". He describes "Predatory Plutocracy" as a nation that ignores individual concerns for the good of business, which is similar to a nation that suppresses individual rights for the good of the state. Both lead to "Oppression and Tyranny."

"Oppression and Tyranny" exists at every level of our federal government, because nobody may question a command or a decision made by upper management. Anyone who questions, or blows the whistle on management decisions, is systematically ostracized or fired. Potential whistleblowers are also eliminated by giving federal jobs to private contractors. AND NOBODY IS HELD ACCOUNTABLE FOR FEDERAL WASTE AND FRAUD.

To guard against "Oppression and Tyranny", ALL AMERICANS, especially federal employees, must demand "FREEDOM OF EXPRESSION", which is protected by the First Amendment of the United States Constitution. "FREEDOM OF EXPRESSION" includes FREEDOM OF SPEECH, FREEDOM OF IDEAS, and FREEDOM OF ASSOCIATION, such as in labor unions and other employee associations.

To help prevent "Oppression and Tyranny", Congress passed the 1989 Whistleblower Protection Act and established the Office of Special Counsel (OSC) as a separate organization to protect federal employees who report waste or fraud. But the failure of the Whistleblower Protection Act only leads to further "Oppression" and persecution of whistleblowers.

Most terrifying, is that the critical federal agencies, such as the Central Intelligence Agency, the Defense Intelligence Agency, the National Security Agency, the General Accounting Office, and others, are excluded from OSC jurisdiction and the 1989 Whistleblower Protection Act. If these critical agencies are denied "FREEDOM OF EXPRESSION" will these agencies become similar to the former Russian KGB, which exemplified "Oppression and Tyranny"?

Windisch submitted an Employee Suggestion to "Reorganize Computer Management," whereby computer professionals would be hired to design and implement 'state of the art' computer systems. Windisch's Employee Suggestion and Whistleblower Complaint were both rejected.

On December 18, 1998, his congressman wrote to Windisch, "...There is no action I can take to investigate or assist you with this issue..."

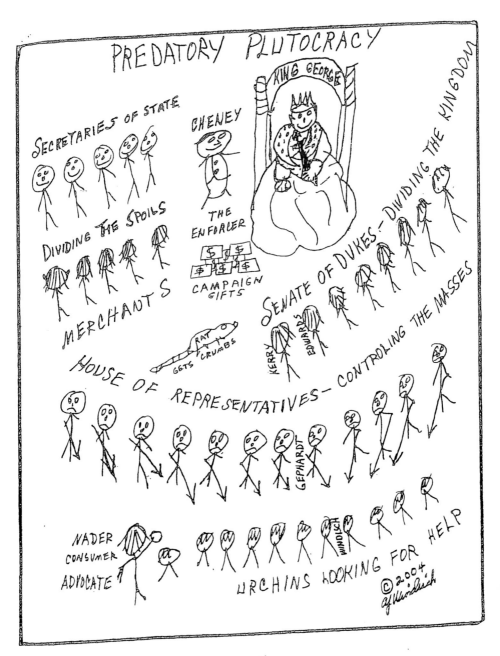

Congress Sounds Alarm

During 200 8, while members of Congress aimlessly complain about China "HACKING" into congressional computers, Congress continues to ignore a 2000 report warning by the General Accountability Office (GAO). "...the potential for more catastrophic damage is significant. Official estimates show that over 100 countries already have or are developing computer attack capabilities. Hostile nations or terrorists could use cyber-based tools and techniques to disrupt military operations, communications networks, and other information systems or networks..."

In May, 2008, I reported to Senator Claire McCaskill about how Congress has created a "NATIONAL SECURITY CRISIS," and I asked her to read my report into the Congressional Record. The public can hear my report at www.NumberBrain.com

Congress Not Accountable

Congress has shown no concern about a 1992 "Financial Management Issues" report by the General Accountability Office (GAO), which describes the federal financial management system as "...essentially a primitive cash budgeting system - without satisfactory controls or audits; without accruals; without balance sheets; without a clear picture of assets, liabilities, returns on investments, or risks..."

This report also points to the solution "...The framework of the CFO (Chief Financial Officers) Act offers great hope for achieving better government management..."

On page 29 of this same report, GAO mistakenly recommends, "...The government could also benefit from more cross-servicing, in which one agency provides financial services to another agency..." Since then, the United States Treasury Department has formed the Financial Management Service (FMS) which provides financial services for most other federal agencies. This commingling of multiple agency funds by the FMS is contrary to the dictates of the CFO ACT, and makes it impossible for Congress to give a true financial accounting to the American people.

National Security Crisis

My name is Anthony (Tony) Windisch.

The U.S. General Accounting Office (GAO) warns all America, about a serious "NATIONAL SECURITY CRISIS," which I will explain in detail.

First, I present an A, B, C, explanation of why we have this NATIONAL SECURITY CRISIS.

A. The American people must learn that the abuse of campaign money not only buys elections, it is plain and simple bribery that influences how our government is run and who gets private contracts.

B. I am a federal whistleblower who spent 20 years and more than $100,000 working for a better government. And, we have a NATIONAL SECURITY CRISIS, because thousands of federal workers, such as me, are not allowed to do their jobs to eliminate government waste and fraud. In fact, workers who report waste or fraud are persecuted by the failure of the 1989 Whistleblower Protection Act.

And

C. I contend, "A nation that ignores individual concerns for the good of business, is the same as the nation that suppresses individual rights for the good of the state. This is how campaign money is destroying our nation."

Our National Security Crisis has many parts which I will explain under individual headings. Then, I will present my conclusion, and give a Solution.

MISMANAGEMENT OF FEDERAL FUNDS

When it comes to federal accounting, the U.S. General Accounting Office (GAO) is the congressional "WATCH-DOG," but this GAO "WATCH-DOG" has no teeth, and Congress no longer listens to its "BARK."

GAO strongly warned in "FINANCIAL MANAGEMENT ISSUES," "Widespread financial management weaknesses are crippling the ability of our leaders to effectively run the federal government."

In this same report, financial mismanagement is clearly described, "The Director of OMB (Office of Management and Budget) described the federal financial management system as "essentially a primitive cash budgeting system–without satisfactory controls or audits; without accruals; without balance sheets; without a clear picture of assets, liabilities, returns on investment, or risks."

Because of this widespread commingling of federal funds, every federal program is at risk of failure, including Social Security, and the Indian Trust Funds.

In 1998, GAO reported that its first ever audit of our nation's consolidated financial statements was an "unmitigated disaster". And evidently, nobody knows the true financial condition of our nation.

Everyone must read the editorial, "Government loses tract of its money," by James K. Glassman.

MISMANAGEMENT OF FINANCIAL INSTITUTIONS

There were warnings about mismanagement of financial institutions from high ranking government officials.

Federal Reserve Board Chairman Alan Greenspan warned that the lines between banks, financial institutions and commercial firms are rapidly blurring, boosting the need for regulatory oversight.

A Director from the Treasury's Office of Financial Institutions Policy, warned Congress, "Some have raised concerns that larger and larger mergers may create institutions that would be considered "too big to fail" if they were threatened with insolvency, increasing the pressure on the Government to protect uninsured depositors and other creditors from loss in order to avoid systemic risk."

Americans sorrowfully remember the Savings & Loans fiasco which cost taxpayers $485 billion. But most Americans are unaware how many uninsured millionaires received a big chunk of this tax money because the U.S. Treasury determined that their bank was "too big to fail."

In spite of these warnings, Congress passed "Banking Reform" which allows more bigger banks. In addition, this bill ignores the concerns of Alan Greenspan by permitting the merger of banks, brokerage, and insurance institutions.

Everyone should read the editorial, "Big banks say they're merging just to serve little old you," by Molly Ivins.

COMPUTER MISMANAGEMENT

I claim that beginning with the 1980 Paperwork Reduction Act, federal accountants have kept computer professionals out of the federal government. As a result, computer waste and fraud has already cost the taxpayers a trillion dollars. And continues with more than $50 billion wasted each year.

My Whistleblower disclosures about computer mismanagement and poor computer security are documented in my book, *Government Computers Add to Waste—Mass Conspiracy to Defraud.*

And a GAO "Computer Chaos" report lists 249 computer projects that failed. I worked on one of these failed projects at the U.S. Department of Agriculture (USDA), "In addition, after spending over $500 million modernizing its financial management systems, the effort was stopped before completion after management found out it did not really know what it was getting from its investment and the systems would not provide for effective oversight and fraud detection."

Years prior, I asked my Congressman to stop this wasteful $500 million project at USDA. My Congressman arranged a meeting with an Assistant Administrator. When this Assistant Administrator questioned his boss about my Complaint, the Assistant Administrator was fired.

GAO sent their report to Congress, "ADP MODERNIZATION Half-Billion Dollar FmHA Effort Lacks Adequate Planning and Oversight." But the House subcommittee did not allow me to testify, and allowed this wasteful project to continue.

NON-EXISTENT COMPUTER CONTROLS

Also reported in "COMPUTER CHAOS," "While the Department of Agriculture was responsible for over $60 billion of taxpayer money last year, OMB states that these funds are at risk for loss or being spent in the wrong way due to unreliable computer generated management information."

While rewriting the computer program that printed this management information, I discovered that this computer file, containing information for $60 billion in farm loans, did not contain a Control Total record. And this computer loan file was not balanced to the General Ledger file on a daily basis as was required. This shows how government computer files do not contain Internal Computer Controls.

In addition, I complained that the wasteful half-billion dollar project was using an "OPEN" Database System, which makes Computer Access Control almost impossible.

In my 1991 Whistleblower Complaint I warned, that the use of an "OPEN" Database System would "unlock" the USDA computers for easy access by computer "hackers." And in May of 2000, GOA confirmed, "almost every federal agency has poor computer security."

FEDERAL COMPUTER HACKERS

I explain Hackers and Computer Security Controls with a true story. Many years ago at an orphan picnic, I went to see the treasurer about obtaining start-up change. I found the cashier's door unlocked. (This is like having no Computer Access Control.) When I opened the door, there was nobody inside. (This is like having no Computer Internal Control.) And a bank bag full of money was on top of the desk.

I became frightened that this orphan money can be so easily stolen. I emptied the bag of money on the desk top, where I also left a note "KILROY WAS HERE." Then I left the room locking the door behind me.

The "LOVEBUG" virus invasion of federal computers shows that federal computers are unlocked. Without computer Internal Controls and since hacker thieves will not leave "KILROY" or "LOVEBUG" notes, nobody can know if or what is being stolen from our national treasury.

GAO reported to Congress in 2000, "As noted in previous testimonies and reports, almost every federal agency has poor computer security. Federal agencies are not only at risk from computer virus attacks, but are also at serious risk of having their key systems and information assets compromised or damaged from both computer hackers as well as unauthorized insiders."

BUSINESS AND INTERNATIONAL COMPUTER HACKERS

GAO report 2000 warned about business and world-wide hackers. "In addition to hitting most federal agencies...the worm/virus affected large corporations, such as AT&T, TWA, and Ford Motor Company; media outlets, such as the *Washington Post,* Dow Jones, ABC News; state governments; school systems; and credit unions, among many others, forcing them to take their networks off-line for hours."

"Internationally, the virus affected businesses, organizations, and governments, including the International Monetary Funds, the British Parliament, Belgium's Banking system, and companies in the Baltics, Denmark, Italy, Germany, Norway, the Netherlands, Sweden, and Switzerland."

When the G-8 industrial nations held an emergency meeting about world-wide hackers, they looked to the United States for leadership. And the United States representative suggested that they must depend on the business/corporate community to solve these problems.

Meanwhile, in the "dog eat dog" business/corporate world, new and old Internet and Telecommunications companies are competing and fighting for turf and air space, which is making a more tangled mess of data communications, and creating an open playground for computer hackers.

HACKERS AND NATIONAL SECURITY

GAO report 2000 continues, "However, the potential for more catastrophic damage is significant. Official estimates show that over 100 countries already have or are developing computer attack capabilities. Hostile nations or terrorists could use cyber-based tools and techniques to disrupt military operations, communications networks, and other information systems or networks."

During the Persian Gulf War, it was reported that a group of Dutch computer hackers offered Iraq their services to help snarl the pentagon electronic communications network.

A news report shows, "Hackers penetrate Pentagon 160,000 times a year."

Another news report, "Hackers invaded a Navy computer and got missile-related software."

Today, there are private contracts to build Navy airplanes, but it would be unthinkable to award "the responsibility and risk of operating and maintaining Navy airplanes" to a private company.

And yet, regardless of numerous federal hacker problems, the Navy awarded EDS a $9 billion contract for "the responsibility and risk of operating and maintaining its entire network of computer systems."

Remembering the horrible events of September 11, and the questions about "airport security," is Congress authorized to give "the responsibility and risk" for National Security to a private company?

GOVERNMENT RESPONSE TO PROBLEMS

Our federal government has spent four years and millions of dollars trying to cover-up financial mismanagement and hacker attacks on Indian Trust Funds. For more information log on at www.indiantrust.com.

To know how congressional committees deal with financial mismanagement problems, read the editorial "Government loses track of its money." We find that at the subcommittee hearing about government's disastrous financial audit, only the conscientious chairman plus one freshman member were in attendance. Shouldn't our congressmen be there to find out where our money went?

On the other hand, we read in "Big banks say they're merging just to serve little old you," that in two years time, members of the Senate and House banking committees received more than $7.8 million in campaign donations from the financial services industry. I'll bet they had packed committee meetings. And I wonder if anyone represented little old you or any individuals?

My Congressman advised, "This will acknowledge receipt of your recent letter regarding your Whistleblower Complaint from many years ago. As you know, you contacted the appropriate agencies and committees regarding this matter some time ago.

"There is no action I can take to investigate or assist you with this issue. Since you are dissatisfied with the Office of the Special Counsel's handling of this matter I can only reiterate that you seek legal counsel for advice regarding any recourse that might be available." I wrote to the Attorney General, who also refused to investigate.

CONCLUSION

In Chapter Eleven of my book, I speculate about filing a Whistle-blower Class Action against the United States Congress. Since then, U.S. General Accountability Office (GAO) has disclosed a serious National Security Crisis, which demands prompt action. And I now realize that the Office of Special Counsel is not the solution but a creation of Congress, therefore Congress must be part of the solution.

During the past twenty years, I did my patriotic duty working for the American people.
Now, it is up to you, the American people to help me, yourselves and America.

Thank you, and God Bless America.

www.NumberBRAIN.com

www.whistleblower.org

CHAPTER ONE
MASS CONSPIRACY TO MISMANAGE

In 1991, while working for the U.S. Department of Agriculture, Anthony Windisch filed a Whistleblower Complaint about gross waste and gross mismanagement of information resources and technology.

Beginning with the Paperwork Reduction Act of 1980, Windisch claims that the federal government has already wasted fifteen years and approaching a trillion dollars on failed attempts to develop efficient and reliable computer systems and controls.

A 1992 General Accounting Office report titled *Financial Management Issues* confirms this complaint. "Widespread financial management weaknesses are crippling the ability of our leaders to effectively run the federal government...financial systems and controls are unreliable...Not only does the government do an abysmal job of rudimentary bookkeeping, but it is also far from having the modern financial systems one would expect of a superpower."

Under the Paperwork Reduction Act, federal systems accountants were told to continue their job of supervising and implementing computer automation systems. Certified Computing Professionals (CCP), who are engineers of office efficiency, were not hired to design integrated computer systems.

Federal accountants remain fearful that computer professionals will replace them, and that computer automation will eliminate the accountants jobs of manual accounting and manual audits. An adversarial battle waged by federal accountants fighting the intrusion of computer automation has prevailed.

In 1984, an Information Resources Management (IRM) supervisor in the Agriculture Department received national honors from the Association of Government Accountants (AGA) for adopting Life Cycle Methodology (LCM) procedures as a guide for the design and implementation of integrated computer systems.

These LCM procedures show how Phase E "General Design" is the critical and most important task, because this is where the basic system design concept is born and where cost/benefit analysis is performed. The U.S. General Accounting

Office (GAO) reports, that throughout the federal government there is inadequate planning and no "General Design" to show cost/benefit justification.

In 1991, the General Accounting Office verified the Windisch Complaint about inadequate planning and no "General Design" with its report, *ADP MODERNIZATION Half-Billion Dollar FmHA Effort Lacks Adequate Planning and Oversight*.

Government-wide mismanagement of IRM is also shown by a 1993 General Services Administration (GSA) book titled, *Information Resources Management Strategic Planning Guide*. This guide gives an example of planning to build a $500,000 house, but there is no hint nor example of "General Design" planning for building integrated housing.

In 1994 Senator William Cohen called attention to the continuing absence of "General Design" and inadequate planning. He reported, "...since 1990 GAO published seventy-four reports about failures of information technology programs, consistently identifying problems with requirements analysis, program management, and cost/benefit analysis."

Unfortunately, while the 1995 extension of the Paperwork Reduction Act casts the blame for unreliable systems and controls in several different directions, the Act does not address nor correct the root cause for unreliable systems and controls.

Then in 1997, the IRS Assistant Commissioner reported that the new IRS computer system does not work and is beyond repair. Yes, another $4 billion wasted on another failed computer project.

Also in 1997, the Health and Human Services Department canceled its multimillion-dollar contract for a new computer system that was supposed to help eliminate Medicare fraud. Officials said the canceled computer contract was behind schedule, over budget, and plagued with problems.

This mass conspiracy to mismanage the federal government still prevails.

Financial Officers Lose Control

Federal officers have lost control of our country's financial management. They are unable to balance financial statements, they do not know what has happened, and they are unaware of how much money is lost or stolen. Unfortunately, neither the Inspector Generals nor the General Accounting Office has any clue about what is happening.

In 1980, financial officers first lost control when their department was stripped of personnel who were responsible for financial management policy and procedures for implementing computer systems. This policy and procedures group formed the nucleus for a separate division of Information Resources Management (IRM), which is now responsible for computer automation policy and procedures for implementing computer systems.

While IRM knew nothing about computer automation policy, IRM continually fought with financial officers about who was responsible for financial management policy.

The 1990 Chief Financial Officer Act confirmed who has the responsibility for financial management. But prior to 1990, IRM's hasty implementation of new computer systems with unreliable controls already befuddled financial officers.

A classic example is the serious problem of unreliable controls at Farmers Home Administration (FmHA) of Agriculture, which is responsible for servicing $50 billion in farm loans.

Prior to 1980, when FmHA processed more than 100,000 loan transactions a day, daily Input to Output (I/O) balancing was performed to assure that the total of loans recorded on the computer file matched the total of Loans Receivable on the General Ledger file. And when the daily processing of loan transactions was completed, the computer file was locked safely in a vault to avoid tampering.

After 1980, IRM shortened this daily transaction processing cycle by no longer reading the entire computer loan file into the system. This meant that daily I/O balancing of total loans on the computer file to the General Ledger was discontinued. In addition, this computer file is no longer locked in a security vault. In fact, it is on line with thousands of authorized users, plus millions of "hackers" who can gain access and modify data. With these unreliable controls, nobody knows how much money is lost or stolen.

The Inspector Generals and the General Accounting Office all seem unaware of what is happening, and they do not acknowledge our country's financial management crisis.

Financial Management Nightmare

The devastating failure of the information revolution will soon turn into a financial management nightmare.

The first ten years of the Paperwork Reduction Act, which began in 1980, has created a generation of inefficient and unreliable computer systems and controls.

While new computer systems have eliminated tons of manual paperwork, they also created mountains of sometimes inefficient computer generated reports. Most alarming, accounting audit trails of manual paperwork were eliminated without being replaced by computer Internal Controls. And federal financial management now finds they are unable to balance our nation's financial statements.

The Chief Financial Officers Act of 1990 reestablished financial management's responsibility for fiscal policy and financial statements. But the failure of Information Resources Management (IRM) and the problem of unreliable systems and controls has not been addressed nor corrected.

I worked for the U.S. Department of Agriculture, and I learned that IRM had no idea about how to design efficient and reliable computer systems. In 1987, I filed an employee suggestion to reorganize information resources management where computer professionals are put in charge of the design and implementation of computer systems. I followed all known administrative procedures in order to be heard, but there was no investigation of my suggestion.

I then discovered that unreliable systems and controls was a government-wide problem. The President's Council on Integrity and Efficiency in 1988 released a report sharply critical of unreliable controls. All ten of the federal computer centers surveyed were found to have inadequate controls. Without ways to check to see if data may have been wrongfully altered, such problems as theft, destruction of data, unauthorized disbursements and financial hardship for millions of federal program participants can all occur.

Inspector General Leon Snead from Agriculture participated in this 1988 President's Council report. He stated that corrective action had been taken on all Agriculture audit recommendations in the 1988 report. But he showed no interest in investigating my 1991 Whistleblower Complaint about the continuing absence of computer Internal Controls throughout the Department of Agriculture.

In my Whistleblower Complaint, I disclosed that Agriculture cannot balance its loans receivable General Ledger account to the computer files, because there are no Internal Control totals on the computer files. And that the absence of computer Internal Controls is a government-wide problem.

The Office of Special Counsel (OSC) held no hearings with me to discuss the disclosures of my Whistleblower Complaint. And my critical disclosure about the absence of computer Internal Controls was not understood, as is evident by an OSC rejection letter dated August 27, 1992, which stated, "You identified your disclosures as your suggestions over the years for improving the agency's security system for computer programs."

This type of system is the *only* possible Internal Control used for outdated batch processing computer systems. My complaint *does not* question the security system for computer programs.

In response to my request for a Senate investigation, Eleanor J. Hill, Chief Counsel for the Permanent Subcommittee on Investigations, suggested I contact Mr. Jack L. Brock, at the General Accounting Office (GAO).

Mr. Brock, (Director—Policy and Issues) reviewed the disclosures of my complaint. Mr. Brock said GAO had made similar observations which have been reported to the president and to congress. And he sent me eight confirming GAO reports.

One of these GAO reports, a 1992 transition report titled *Financial Management Issues* identifies the problems:

> Widespread financial management weaknesses are crippling the ability of our leaders to effectively run the federal government...financial systems and controls are unreliable. Breakdowns in financial systems and controls not only waste billions of dollars, but also reinforce the deeply rooted public perception that the government cannot effectively manage the taxpayers' money.

GAO also complained about a backlog of several thousand requests for manual audits of government assets. It is evident that even GAO does not fully understand the need for computer Internal Controls that can provide for automatic computer audits.

Serious questions have been raised about the security of government computers. To show the problem, I call attention to a news headline "Russian Hackers Steal $10 Million Out Of Citibank." This headline illustrates that non-government Citibank had adequate Internal Controls, because the hackers were discovered and identified. On the other hand, federal computers have unreliable systems and controls. Therefore our government cannot know if hackers have invaded, and cannot know what is missing or stolen.

Federal computer controls are so bad that even people without computers are stealing from the government. Theft was so widespread during the IRS Rapid Refund Scam, that investigators were told not to look into thefts of less than $10,000. Unreliable controls even allow Social Security and other government checks to be stolen and cashed without detection.

Stories continue about unreliable systems and controls throughout government. During a sample audit of the Pentagon, Senator John Glenn found one thousand accounts payable errors. Government even tried to give our money away. Fortunately contractors returned $1.4 billion in overpayments. Senator Glenn said, "I am concerned that we are just looking at the tip of a very large iceberg."

To illustrate unreliable controls, a GAO audit for years 1978-86 showed a $65 billion difference between Social Security taxes collected as reported by the Social Security Administration (SSA) and the Internal Revenue Service (IRS). If GAO looked further, GAO would probably find that a third different amount of Social Security taxes had actually reached the U.S. Treasury.

These unreliable controls of payroll tax collection will get worse after January 1997, when businesses will be required to transmit their payroll taxes directly to one of five large banks. Businesses will lose the assurance and control of making payroll tax deposits at their local banks.

Meanwhile, one congressional committee is still trying to figure out what went wrong to cause the Savings and Loan fiasco, which cost the taxpayers $481 billion. And without concern about GAO's financial management issues, another congressional committee is working rapidly to deregulate the banking industry.

If government has no idea about controlling its own financial management systems, how can government effectively monitor the five or six mega-banks that will soon control our country? We are surely heading for a financial management nightmare.

Need for More Bank Regulation

In April, 1997, at the Chicago Fed's conference on bank structure and competition, Federal Reserve Board Chairman Alan Greenspan said, "The lines between banks, financial institutions, and commercial firms are rapidly blurring, boosting the need for regulatory oversight.

"It's pretty apparent that the dividing line which segregates commerce and finance and finance and banking will continuously erode as the technology increases... Sometime out in the future...we will have a terribly difficult time making judgments about what is commerce and what is finance."

Greenspan's speech focused on the need for regulation under the changing environment to ensure bank safety and soundness.

On May 2, 1997, Windisch wrote to Mr. Greenspan, "I am writing to reinforce your warning about the need for more bank regulation.

"The attached summary of my story *Financial Management Nightmare*, concludes, "If government has no idea about controlling its own financial management systems, how can government effectively monitor the five or six mega banks that will soon control our country? We are surely heading for a financial management nightmare.

"I have enclosed my book of testimony to substantiate my horror story."

CHAPTER TWO
FINANCIAL MANAGEMENT CRISIS

Financial Management Issues

© 1997 *WINDISCH*

"Computers Cause Problems"

On May 6, 1997, Windisch again wrote to President Clinton, "My attached correspondence with Alan Greenspan shows the reality of the pending *financial management nightmare.*

"*You have not answered* any of my critical letters in this regard, including the following: May 1, 1997, February 10, 1997, January 31, 1997, January 10, 1997, October 18, 1996, April 26, 1996.

"Have my concerns fallen on deaf ears?"

The Windisch letter of *April 26, 1996,* is reprinted in the last chapter titled "Solution to End Computer Chaos."

A December 1992 transition report (GAO/OCG-93-4TR) by the General Accounting Office, titled *Financial Management Issues* sends a warning with its opening statement on page 4, "Widespread financial management weaknesses are crippling the ability of our leaders to effectively run the federal government. Reducing the federal deficit requires monumentally difficult decisions. If our government is to make these decisions in an informed manner, it must have better financial information."

'First, financial data are often inadequate or erroneous. Our financial audits of various agencies regularly identify tens of billions of dollars in accounting errors as well as serious gaps in information. These problems undermine the government's ability to effectively perform basic financial management functions, make informed decisions, and conduct adequate oversight of taxpayers' funds.

"Second, financial systems and controls are unreliable. Breakdowns in financial systems and controls not only waste billions of dollars, but also reinforce the deeply rooted public perception that the government cannot effectively manage the taxpayers' money.

"Third, results oriented reports on financial condition and operating performance are largely nonexistent. While the government has a flood of cash based information, it has collected few data to monitor the cost of programs and measure their performance.

"Not only does the government do an abysmal job of rudimentary bookkeeping, but it is also far from having the modern financial systems one would expect of a superpower."

For example, GAO says earnings data reported to the Social Security Administration and the IRS for the 1978 to 1986 tax years show a difference of about $65 billion.

And according to this same GAO report, unreliable systems and controls are also "...contributing to the billions of dollars in losses in the government's portfolio of over $850 billion in loans and loan guarantees is the fact that fundamental information programs are all too often lacking or unreliable."

Reform Urgently Needed

Still quoting from *Financial Management Issues*, "The Chief Financial Officers Act tries to address such problems by requiring the development of integrated systems.

"Once a budget has been enacted, the financial focus shifts primarily to the next year's budget. How the money was spent and what results were achieved are secondary.

"Fundamental reform is urgently needed. Without decisive action now, efforts to reform financial management and to fix current high-risk areas will falter, and the government will be increasingly vulnerable to new losses."

GAO Report Gives Bad Advice

While GAO reports that many recommended financial audits by various agencies are overdue, they do not recognize the need for internal computer controls which can provide for the generation of automatic computer audits.

Alarmingly, in *Financial Management Issues* on page 29, GAO recommends the mass production and merging of similar financial systems. "The government could also benefit from more cross-servicing, in which one agency provides financial services to another agency. Today, for instance, the Department of Agriculture provides payroll services to about 40 other agencies."

This commingling of agency payroll funds along with unreliable financial controls and reports invites disaster as inadequate controls hide theft, fraud, and waste.

The Pentagon followed this same GAO recommendation to merge like financial systems, and the Defense Finance and Accounting Services (DFAS) now provide Accounts Payable services for many different Pentagon agencies.

As a result of this mass production of accounts payable checks, manual paperwork was eliminated, including paperwork audit trails. A spot-audit in 1994 of nine contractors by the GAO uncovered one thousand mistakenly issued payments that were returned to the Defense Finance and Accounting Service. And during the first nine months of 1993, defense contractors returned $1.4 billion in overpayments to the Pentagon.

Senator John Glenn was quoted as saying, "Given the magnitude of waste in this small sample, I am concerned that we are just looking at the tip of a very large iceberg."

"Government Computers Add to Waste" by Anthony J. Windisch
(published in the *St. Louis Post-Dispatch* April 30, 1993)

The Clinton administration, with a panel headed by Vice President Al Gore, is looking for ways to cut government waste. Federal employees have been asked to get involved. But members of the J. Peter Grace organization, Citizens Against Government Waste, wonder why more suggestions are needed, since the Grace Commission, almost a decade ago delivered 2,478 recommendations in its proclaimed "war on waste."

The Grace Commission recommendation for computer automation, however, has proven to be a massive federal fiasco. Computer automation--done the way the federal government did it--has cost taxpayers money, rather than helped savings. I estimate that as much as $500 billion may well have been lost or wasted due to (1) under-utilized computer equipment, (2) failed and inefficient computer systems, (3) manual paperwork, plus computer paperwork, (4) lack of computer automated services where they could be effective, and (5) inadequate controls and chaotic accounting.

Under the Paperwork Reduction Act, federal systems accountants were assigned the job of supervising and designing computer automation. Certified computer professionals, who are engineers of office efficiency, were not hired. And an adversarial battle waged by federal accountants fighting the intrusion of computer automation has prevailed.

My nine years of experience working under the supervision of government systems accountants was a frustrating and frightening study of gross waste and inadequate financial controls. Numerous General Accounting Office reports show computer automation failures throughout the federal government. Other audits show that government operations in general are hampered by inefficient computer systems.

Besides inefficient computer systems, the president's Council on Integrity and Efficiency in 1988 released a report sharply critical of the systems' controls. All ten of the federal computer centers surveyed were found to have inadequate controls. Without ways to check to see if data may have been tampered with, such problems as theft, destruction of data, unauthorized disbursements and financial hardship for millions of federal program participants can all occur. Six of these 10 centers collectively disburse an estimated $273 billion, and eight are part of financial systems that controlled more than $1.4 trillion in assets.

During the House of Representatives bank scandal, the bank computer system must have had adequate controls because investigators were able to learn who wrote the overdrafts. Without adequate computer controls, there would have been no audit trail and no way to find out what happened to the money. Without adequate controls, our government cannot even be aware that money is missing.

A recent *Dateline* exposé of the IRS Rapid Refund scam wherein people created fake W-2s to get undeserved refunds is a clear demonstration of what can happen when controls are inadequate. The IRS was unaware that money was stolen.

In the past, a *60 Minutes* exposé showed a bogus army colonel who cashed more than $3 million of bogus checks in one year. This also demonstrates the danger of inadequate controls, as the government does not know if this type of theft is continuing.

And for more than 10 years at the Farmers Home Administration where I worked, our government has not been aware of the total volume of farm loan repayments that are continuously stolen.

Inefficient computer systems and inadequate controls also lead to impossible audits. Government accounting is, at best, chaotic. Our government's chief financial officer does not know and cannot know the true financial condition of our country.

The value of good computer systems and adequate controls can be seen in the space program. During a flight to Venus for example, a good computer system includes numerous check points when the exact location is told; and adequate controls show what adjustments are necessary to reach the planet.

With government's inefficient computer systems and chaotic accounting, at the end of the month or at other critical check points, no one knows where we are financially. During the 1992 presidential campaign for example, when asked about the size of our budget deficit, the Bush administration could only guess that it would probably be somewhere around the $250 billion originally projected. By the time of the presidential debates, the budget deficit reached $290 billion and was still increasing. I still wonder what the final deficit amount was for 1992. Unfortunately, with chaotic government accounting, nobody knows the true financial condition of this nation, though it is in economic trouble. Although President Bill Clinton cannot be blamed for what has happened during prior administrations, he cannot continue to ignore this chaotic government accounting and the tremendous amount of government waste.

Clinton must recognize his responsibility. His priorities should be (1) correct the chaotic government accounting, (2) establish computer financial controls, (3) create good computer systems, (4) cut the cost of government bureaucracy and (5) eliminate government waste.

I think he should also demand a balanced budget, but neither he nor many federal agencies can know how well they are doing in trying to reduce the deficit unless they do the first five points.

Clinton promised to cut the budget deficit in half in four to five years. And for every dollar in new spending, he said he would eliminate $2 of government waste. We have yet to see this promise turned into sound proposals, and until the federal government increases the efficiency and audit ability of its computer systems, billions will continue to be wasted.

The Gore panel, which was commissioned to eliminate waste, must get to the heart of the computer fiasco if it is to have any success.

CHAPTER THREE
UNRELIABLE CONTROLS = IMPOSSIBLE AUDITS

'It's One Deep, Black Hole'

Feds Can Audit Without Internal Controls?

In 1988 the President's Council warned that all ten federal computer centers surveyed had inadequate controls that could lead to theft and unauthorized disbursements.

Computer financial systems must have two types of controls: External Controls that consist of input/output balancing and other auditing methods that are performed around or external to the computer; and Internal Controls that can be automatically performed by or internal to the computer.

For large computer systems, External Controls which are labor intensive, by themselves are usually inadequate or not cost efficient; therefore Internal Controls are needed to assist by providing automatic computer auditing.

One example of the need for Internal Controls is the Program Loan Accounting System (PLAS) at Farmers Home Administration (FmHA) of the U.S. Department of Agriculture (USDA).

I have disclosed that there are *no Internal Controls* for this PLAS computer loan file!

To have Internal Controls there must be Control Totals. For over ten years, ever since the IDMS PLAS loan file was created, there have been *no Control Totals* on this file. Whenever the contents of this PLAS file are added together, without a Control Total against which to compare, it can not be known if the new total is correct. Also, without Control Totals there can not be automatic computer auditing of the PLAS file.

Because PLAS is a large computer system and the use of External Controls alone requires extensive manual work, it is next to impossible to conduct a successful audit of the PLAS loan file. Therefore, Internal Controls are needed in order to assist by performing more frequent and automatic computer audits, to decrease the manual audit work, and to obtain an absolute audit balance.

How do the feds perform audits without internal controls?

How can the feds guard our treasury without internal controls?

Conspiracy to Defraud

While working for the Department of Agriculture from 1982 to 1991, all my efforts to establish reliable financial controls for the $50 billion farm loan program were ignored and rejected. And unreliable controls continue to cause waste and hide theft.

Prior to 1980, a computer tape file containing loan records had a trailer record which contained financial Control Totals. And this computer file for Loans Receivable was balanced daily with the financial General Ledger.

After 1982, when this computer Loans Receivable file was converted to an integrated disk file, financial Control Totals were no longer maintained. (Imagine not keeping a Control Total in your banking check book.) And daily balancing of the Computer Loans Receivable to the General Ledger was discontinued.

In May 1984 after more newspaper stories about the theft of loan payments, I wrote to the Systems Control Branch, FmHA:

> ...I was manager of Computer Operations at Boatmen's Bank, where I was also responsible for Demand Deposit and Lock Box balancing and control....I submitted six different Employee Suggestions in an attempt to point out the lack of control in several areas at Farmers Home Administration. My suggestions were not discussed with me, and were rejected.

During 1984-85, I worked on the Automated Program Delivery System (APDS) which was designed as an online computer system which would detect and eliminate the theft of loan payments. During this review of the APDS system, I recommended the use of control records to maintain financial Control Totals. These internal computer Control Totals would be used to balance the computer file of Loans Receivable with the financial General Ledger. These Control Totals would also provide for automatic computer audits. Unfortunately the APDS system with its Internal Controls was not implemented.

The APDS project failed for many reasons, one of which was the fact that Input to Output balancing procedures were non-existent.

On April 2, 1986, I wrote to my team leader:

> A basic element of the APDS detail system design is incomplete. A transaction to General Ledger Balancing matrix is very incomplete and practically non-existent. ...Without the completion of this balancing matrix it is impossible to have an Update Transaction to General Ledger walk through that is necessary to verify the validity of the Data Base content and individual program specifications.

While working on the APDS system I also learned that Agriculture uses an unacceptable accounting practice by allowing unlimited numbers of reverse and repost transactions. And many transactions cross multiple accounting periods to further complicate account balancing. One year there were six accounts that each had more than 950 transactions for the year. Some of these multiple transactions were backdated ten years.

A bank examiner said whenever he saw multiple transactions he was obligated to investigate. He explained that hiding an object behind a single tree is easy to find, but if that tree is in a forest of trees you may never find the object.

I submitted Employee Suggestion FC-301 "Provide Better Audit Trail" recommending the use of a single "Memo Post" transaction, which would show the net result of multiple reverse/repost transactions. This single transaction would have a plus or minus interest amount offset by a like amount of minus or plus principal, giving a net zero additional payment received. My suggestion was not discussed with me and it was rejected.

Then while working on the loan transaction history files, I compared the total of payment history to an annual 1987 financial report. I was shocked to learn that the history payment total was over $4 billion more than the $7.4 billion listed as collections on the financial report.

In 1987 I submitted Suggestion #87 "Guard Against Computer Hackers," for controlling farm loans and payments. My suggestion was accepted as a good idea, but it was not discussed with me, and it was not implemented.

Meanwhile, in order to track lost or stolen payments, the Office of Inspector General (OIG) instructed the agency to implement a computerized Deposit Fund system. This system was designed to match loan payments against loan account updates, and print an unmatched Deposit Fund Listing which would then be reconciled.

A November 1989 OIG audit of the Deposit Fund system states, "THE FMHA GENERAL LEDGER AND DETAIL DEPOSIT FUND ARE NOT BEING RECONCILED."

In 1989, stolen, lost, and incorrect payments coupled with delinquent payments caused such a large backlog of litigation and pending foreclosures of farm properties that congress allocated $600 million in a *failed* attempt to reconcile this deplorable condition.

Adding to Agriculture's chaotic accounting, FmHA implemented a hideous Interest Subsidy Recapture plan. This elaborate Interest Subsidy Recapture scheme creates unnecessary fake Interest Subsidy payment records. These pseudo-Interest Subsidy records are automatically applied three days after the regular loan payment due date. Three days of interest is calculated with the remainder credited to loan principal. Subsidy Interest and Subsidy Principal totals are separately accumulated on the loan account record, in order to regain (Recapture) the Interest Subsidy whenever a loan is in default.

The way in which this Interest Subsidy Recapture plan was implemented is *wasteful, unreliable, and conceals waste and theft.*

A November 1990 letter from State Director James L Howe to Mr. LaVerne Ausman, Administrator, Farmers Home Administration, states in part,

"I wanted to bring you up to date on the embezzlement at our Omaha county office....In addition, we have verified that an additional $500 was taken during October using the same method....My concern is that this same problem could occur in any of our offices nationwide."

The camouflage use of pseudo-Subsidy payments is evident, "The main problem, as I see it, is Form FmHA 451-2 'Schedule of Remittances' of interest subsidy recapture."

On September 23, 1993, I received a letter from James R. Ebbitt, USDA Office of Inspector General stating,

"...we agree that Farmers Home Administration (FmHA) National Finance Center in St. Louis needs to improve controls over computer processing and financial systems. Our audit of the FmHA fiscal year 1992 financial statements (enclosed) found that internal control structure problems affected FmHA's ability to report financial data...."

In my 1991 Whistleblower Complaint, I disclosed the absence of computer Internal Controls, highlighting the absence of financial Control Totals on the Program Loan Accounting System (PLAS) computer file.

The rejection and response received from both the Office of Special Counsel (OSC), and the Office of Inspector General (OIG), shows that neither OSC, nor OIG understand the meaning nor need for computer Internal Controls.

Unreliable Controls and Chaotic Accounting

In *Financial Management Issues* of 1992, GAO reported about unreliable controls and chaotic accounting throughout government. I will give a sampling of unreliable controls and chaotic accounting at Agriculture.

The loans receivable on the PLAS computer loan file was not being balanced to the General Ledger. And there was inaccurate accountability as a newspaper article cited a 70 percent delinquency risk of farm loans based on total direct loans of $19.5 billion. In contradiction, the 1991 financial report on page three lists "...an insured loan portfolio in excess of $50 billion...." And on page sixteen of this same report is listed yet another contradiction, INSURED LOANS RECEIVABLE 1.3M LOANS $41B. During this same period of time $10 billion of the best performing loans were given away for 30-40 cents on the dollar. Rumor has it that an Under Secretary of Agriculture was on the board of directors for a Savings and Loan that received part of this gift (or theft).

I had my greatest shock when I was assigned the task of rewriting the computer program that printed the Insured Borrowers Delinquency Report. There were no internal computer control totals to account for the amount of loans recorded on the PLAS computer file which was used to print the report.

Following good programming practice, I was compelled to perform an audit of the contents of this loan file. I learned that less than 50 percent of the three million loans on the file were listed on the Delinquency Report as active loans.

Three delinquent loans from California were understated by thirty million dollars in total. I was told that nobody pays attention to large delinquent loans because of political ramifications. One "4H" loan in question was thought to belong to a former California governor.

There were several thousand long time open loans that were not being reported. I learned that most of the open loans were there for more than a year because Congress did not know whether they should be loans or grants.

Other loan records represented acquired property, loans waiting for litigation, asset sales, etc., for which there was no proper accounting.

My experience at Agriculture shows how unreliable systems and controls can contribute to the billions of dollars in losses in the government's portfolio of $850 billion in loans and loan guarantees as reported by GAO in *Financial Management Issues*.

Without prompt attention, this financial management crisis will continually get worse, until it explodes.

While the president and Congress have ignored this crisis, congressional committees are still trying to learn what went wrong with the financial controls to cause the Savings and Loan debacle. A Banking Committee even questions the self-auditing practices of the nation's Federal Reserve Banks. And it is not known how widespread is bank fraud and theft, because of government's unreliable controls.

If government cannot resolve its own internal financial management issues, it is unlikely that government can establish adequate financial controls for bank merger mania. And with unreliable financial controls, mega bank mergers can lead to major bank failures, which will cost the taxpayers hundreds of billions of dollars and bring financial ruin to our country.

CHAPTER FOUR
INFORMATION REVOLUTION NIGHTMARE

National Information Infrastructure (NII) has become a commonplace term to describe the promise of communications networks and more broadly, information technology. The Clinton administration is in awe with cyberspace and the information super highway, while Gingrich and congress struggle with their "Howdy Doody" system of Internet and E-mail. But in contrast, they all have closed their eyes and ears to the serious financial management issues that the General Accounting Office says are caused by unreliable computer systems and controls.

In *Parade* Magazine of February, 1996, Jack Anderson, who joined the late J. Peter Grace to form Citizens Against Government Waste, commented about savings already made, "this multibillion dollar saving has barely skimmed the top scum off the waste that the Grace Commission uncovered."

The *U.S. News & World Report* of January 15, 1996, has an article, "Technology Wasteland," telling about Washington's failure to harness computers.

This story notes Washington has gone from being the driving force behind a nascent computer industry to a technological also-ran. Reports by the General Accounting Office and Senator William Cohen's Oversight of Government Management subcommittee depict a federal government lost in the computer wilderness.

Roger Johnson, the computer czar at the General Services Administration, is also quoted, giving examples of failed information resources management, including, "The Farmers Home Administration manages its loan portfolio with color-coded index cards, despite spending $200 million on computer systems to perform the task."

I worked for Farmers Home Administration (FmHA), U.S. Department of Agriculture, where FmHA was responsible for servicing farm loans totaling more than $50 billion.

The USDA had a dream about a state of the art computer online loan servicing system. Such an ideal system would have online reporting with electronic paging, ABC analysis, and exception item search. This integrated system would also have an Integrated Data Dictionary (IDD) for reference, and information about the availability of government farm loan programs.

Computer online loan servicing will reduce the data input error rate by 80-90 percent. And automatic computer auditing will detect and eliminate the theft of loan payments.

To use this system, a computer inquiry screen will present instructions for access to the computer information. Users can obtain answers about loan policy questions, loan availability, and see current loan account information. The IDD dictionary could be accessed to show the description and meaning of any piece of data within the computer system.

This dream system will automatically collect data for work measurement reports, which will be used for efficiency analysis and managing the work place.

Such an efficient online computer system is designed to give better customer service and permit the closing of 40-50 percent of the three thousand county offices for savings of a *billion dollars* per year.

Efforts to build this dream system started in 1981 when the agency converted its Burroughs computer operating system to an IBM operating system using the Integrated Data Management System (IDMS). Information for a Program Loan Accounting System (PLAS) was loaded onto the IDMS computer database.

This PLAS integrated database system is very inefficient because of its faulty file design, and it cannot be used as an efficient computer online loan servicing system. After more than ten years of wasteful misuse of the PLAS system, there are no plans for design development nor correction of this PLAS system, and this waste continues.

Also in the 1980s, financial management along with program management spent several years and thousands of man-hours working with outside contractors to design an Automated Program Delivery System (APDS) which would provide their dream for a computer online loan servicing system. The APDS system was planned as a redesign of financial management's PLAS system, plus the addition of loan servicing requirements for Program Management. But an uneducated Information Resources Management (IRM) failed in their supervision of design development, and the APDS dream system was never implemented.

In 1991 a Senate committee chastised Agriculture for spending a billion dollars on computer systems for the county offices, which produced little or no savings and the closing of only two offices.

At the same time in 1991, a House committee permitted Agriculture's IRM to continue with the installation of an independent computer system for program management's use in the county offices. The committee ignored the Windisch report about gross mismanagement, and issued a report by GAO titled, "ADP MODERNIZATION Half-Billion Dollar FmHA Effort Lacks Adequate Planning and Oversight."

And an ORACLE integrated computer system was installed for stand-alone use at Agriculture's county offices.

Instead of more efficient loan servicing, the work load at the county offices has increased. Workers continue to write manual reports about daily work activity for work measurement reports. Numerous computer processing tasks have been added to the work load. Computer data entry errors have increased. Current loan account information is difficult to obtain. The theft of loan payments continues. And the ORACLE system provides none of the benefits envisioned by an online loan servicing system. Congress has drastically cut the work force and reduced the number of servicing offices.

At Agriculture, the Information Revolution dream has become a horrible NIGHTMARE. A nightmare that prevails throughout the federal government.

CHAPTER FIVE
UNRELIABLE COMPUTER SYSTEMS

WHO SAID WE NEED A GENERAL DESIGN?

Anthony J. Windisch, CCP

Feds Build Hotels Without General Design?

Building a multi-phase computer system is much like building a multifloor hotel. Our federal government builds multiphase computer systems without using a General Design plan.

The computer data base file is the foundation of the computer system, much like the foundation of the building is to the hotel. A computer system may have five or more phases in its construction, similar to the five floors for the construction of a hotel.

All five floors of a hotel cannot be built simultaneously. First there must be a blueprint or General Design. Before the first floor of the hotel can be built, there must be a foundation. Furthermore that foundation must be able to support all five floors of the hotel.

Imagine the confusion and turmoil if there were no General Design for this hotel. Imagine the fifth floor built first without a foundation. What would happen to this hotel project if all five floors were built on a foundation that could only support three floors?

Farmers Home Administration (FmHA), United States Department of Agriculture (USDA) is making a fourth major attempt to modernize their multiphase computer system--a fourth attempt, again without a General Design plan.

Computer automation problems have historically plagued FmHA. They were again reviewed October 29, 1991, at a House Hearing by the Agriculture Subcommittee. Report GAO/IMTEC92-9, from the U.S. General Accounting Office (GAO), was used to summarize the committee's findings. The title is "ADP MODERNIZATION Half-Billion Dollar FmHA Effort Lacks Adequate Planning and Oversight."

FmHA officials at this hearing blame their computer modernization problems on the prior Assistant Administrator for Management and "promise" to do better. The House Subcommittee, unfortunately, failed to investigate further. Other evidence was submitted to document the need for computer professionals to design FmHA's computer systems. Further, the subcommittee did not question FmHA's project life cycle chart, blatantly missing the General Design function within their system development work cycle. Apparently FmHA will again attempt to build a multiphase computer system without using a General Design plan. Another system destined for failure.

How can the Feds build a hotel without using a General Design?

How can the Feds build a multi-phase computer system without using a General Design?

Without General Design There is Mismanagement

An Information Resources Management (IRM) supervisor received national honors from the Association of Government Accountants (AGA) for adopting Life Cycle Methodology (LCM) procedures for the design and implementation of integrated computer systems.

A critical path scheduling chart for LCM shows how Phase E "General Design" is most important, because here the basic system concept is born, as all subsystems are merged and integrated into one efficient system.

A ROWE consultant report commissioned by the IRM Administrator casts blame for the troubled IRM history on "...an unsophisticated user community and unrealistic expectations." In the past, this was a valid observation, but today's integrated computer systems must be designed during the "General Design" process, using the expertise of computer professionals.

In a July 17, 1989 letter, the IRM administrator responded to the complaint about non-performance of "General Design," "...a task force...is currently identifying a systems development life cycle methodology to be adopted and adhered to...."

As a result of this promise, a JUNE 1990 reissue of "PROJECT LIFE CYCLE" does not even show a "General Design" phase.

Government wide mismanagement of IRM is shown by a 1993 General Services Administration (GSA) book titled *Information Resources Management Strategic Planning Guide*. This guide illustrates planning to build a $500,000 house, but there are no "General Design" plans for building integrated housing such as a hotel.

Numerous reports by the General Accounting Office about IRM failures throughout government, constantly confirm this lack of "General Design" with headlines such as, "ADP MODERNIZATION—Half-Billion Dollar FmHA Effort lacks Adequate Planning and Oversight."

Mismanagement of IRM will continue as long as there is inadequate planning and no "General Design" for integrated computer systems.

Failure After Failure Continues

1. Unified Management Information System (UMIS).

By 1982, when I joined Agriculture's Automated Information Services division, the UMIS system had already failed. In its report (CED-78-68, Feb. 27, 1978), the General Accounting Office (GAO) gave criticism, "Farmers Home Administration Needs To Better Plan, Direct, Develop, and Control Its Computer Based United Management Information System."

2. Conversion to IDMS Database System (CIDS).

In 1982, a Burroughs computer operating system was converted to an IBM computer operating system, along with Conversion to an Integrated IDMS Database System (CIDS).

CIDS had inadequate planning and an improper design of the IDMS database, which had the following results: a) The unplanned design of the IDMS database will not support efficient online computer processing. b) Daily computer updating of some 100,000 transactions requires five passes of this volume of data, when before CIDS only three passes were required. c) Because of faulty database design the Culprit report writing system cannot be efficiently used. d) Instead of correcting the problem, the agency purchased a separate "FOCUS" reporting system, which requires the periodic creation of a redundant and wasteful updated Focus database, which is then used for Focus report writing.

For more than ten years, this gross waste of computer resources has continued, without any plans for development nor correction.

Nobody has reported this CIDS failure to Congress.

3. Automated Program Delivery System (APDS).

In 1984, I was detailed to review the design specifications for the APDS computer system. The design contractor Price Waterhouse (PW) waged a constant battle to overcome agency ignorance of procedures for designing efficient computer systems.

Although APDS was designed to reduce the data entry error rate by 80-90 percent, the agency kept insisting that PW design an automatic reverse/repost system to correct data input errors. a) Automatic error correction is contrary to the designing for the accurate computer online entry of data. b) The agency compounds its problems by using an unacceptable accounting practice of allowing unlimited reverse/repost transactions which cut across multiple accounting periods. Note: I documented this problem with my Employee Suggestion FC-301 "PROVIDE BETTER AUDIT TRAIL." c) In the agency's existing automatic reverse/repost system, the agency uses the unacceptable accounting practice of overlaying new transactions on top of prior transaction history thus wiping out any audit trail.

Then PW designed an Accounts Payable subsystem to be controlled locally, where the agency would warehouse the payables and maintain a Vendor Master file. But the agency insisted that local work must be eliminated and all payables must be sent immediately to the National Finance Office (NFC) in New Orleans for warehousing and payment, without the agency worrying about controls.

Warehousing of payables at the agency was eliminated, and the agency has no way to control nor correct the contents of its accounts payable records being held at NFC. In addition, NFC maintains a vendor file for agency payables, which is not a true control file. The NFC vendor file was designed to comply with IRS regulations for the reporting of yearly accumulated payments of $400 or more. The vendor file is first created from payable records after the records reach NFC.

When the APDS design project was near completion, the agency instructed PW to remove all report documentation from all other subsystems and collectively document them in a single reporting subsystem. I demonstrated that this revision was unnecessary, as I used the Culprit report writer to produce a sequential listing of all reports within the APDS system.

Windisch Evaluation and Commentary

Mr. Windisch made many valuable suggestions to enhance the design of the APDS system. Most notable was his review of the Processing Controls subsystem, when he pointed out the need for financial control totals on the computer loan file. As a consequence, BALHEAD, and BALDTL records were added in order to provide needed controls, and to permit automatic computer audits.

While performing the managerial tasks of reviewing the APDS system designs, Mr. Windisch requested a temporary promotion to Programmer Analyst Grade 12, representing team leader status. Mr. Windisch was denied promotion.

After the PW design contract was completed, I was relegated back to being a member of a Programmer Analyst team. Several Programmer Analyst teams were responsible for working with the Programming Contractor OAO, to help reconcile their programming questions. All design questions were directed to the Systems Accountants who were responsible for ongoing design and system implementation.

During my work with OAO, I accumulated books of design questions that were either unanswered or answered incorrectly. And there were many design problems left unattended.

A computer consulting firm, MITRE, also conducted a review of design and implementation problems. The following is one of their many findings to illustrate the type of problems that had sabotaged the APDS project.

During the General Design phase of APDS, PW had designed a computer master input screen that contained some twenty-four pieces of input data. PW then wrote program specifications, using these twenty-four pieces of input data in its specifications or instructions for writing computer programs. But when OAO tried to follow PW's program specifications, OAO learned that agency accountants had changed the meaning, and created a different set of twenty-five pieces of input data.

Meanwhile, agency Computer Operations people also became frustrated, because they were unable to obtain help for drawing a transaction to general ledger matrix, which was needed in order to write Input/Output balancing procedures. A brief five minute walk-thru meeting was held, and it was learned that the four position identification for transaction records had not been assigned.

The agency systems accountants then proposed using a larger six position identification, rather than using the four position identifier that was already designed for use throughout the APDS system design and in system wide program specifications.

Near the end of the programming contract I had to bite my tongue when I heard that OAO was being sued for their inability to implement Culinet's Online General Ledger system. This Online General Ledger system could not be implemented because the general ledger file organization had not been determined. The agency was redesigning a new general ledger file organization of sub-program within program, to replace the existing general ledger organization of loan fund code within fund entity.

Yes, GAO reported the dismal failure of APDS, but it blamed all the wrong people for its failure.

After getting a bad rap from GAO, it is no wonder that Price Waterhouse closed its St. Louis office for administering government computer automation contracts.

4. Strategic Financial System Improvements (SFSI)

Computer system users picked up the pieces of their critical needs from the failed APDS system, and documented an excellent Users Conceptual Design package, creating the SFSI project plan.

a) I was assigned to Project 4.A.1 Online Borrower History Inquiry, one of the first subsystems to be implemented. On page 4-3.4 of the Users Conceptual Design package for SFSI, the purpose was,

"Online History is used to support field loan servicing." But a subsequent detailed Functional Design Specifications (FDS) showed a different purpose,

"...a means for the technician to see detailed history." The original user requirement was not pursued.

When given the FDS package to begin writing computer programs, I asked for Program Specifications (PS). I was told there were no PSs and I must write my own. Then I asked for Subsystem Design Specifications (SDS), so I could determine how many programs needed to be written. I was told that I would need to plan and design my own SDS. Finally I asked to see a computer Conceptual and/or General Design for the total SFSI project. I needed to see the Conceptual or General Design in order to understand how my assigned Online History subsystem fits into the plans for an integrated SFSI system.

There was no computer Conceptual nor General Design to show how an integrated SFSI system should be built. When I proposed my own computer Conceptual Design for the SFSI system, I was politely told that systems design was not the responsibility of a Programmer Analyst. I then documented my ideas for a Conceptual Design with Employee Suggestion FC-504 "Design and Implement ALSIS."

Without a General Design for the total system which caused inadequate planning, implementation of the Online Borrower History Inquiry did not meet user requirements at the county field offices and must be considered a failure.

b) Project 1-A-1 Job Aid, was assigned to an outside contractor named Kendrick. I believe this subsystem was incorrectly designed as a stand-alone system at the field offices for online entry of loan applications. This project created more waste in the following ways:

- The central Integrated Data Dictionary (IDD) is not being used to identify and define computer data elements.

- Instead of using standard IDD data element names, different data names have been created which cause confusion and additional data entry errors.

- IDD is not being used to develop online computerized loan servicing Policy and Procedures.

- An Office Record on the central computer is not available to automatically collect work measurement records from the county offices.

- More manual records of worker activity are required by the Work Measurement group in order to produce bigger and better Work Measurement reports.

- Since the Work Measurement group is not part of the Computer Automation Division, the work of an independent Work Measurement group is a *complete waste.*

c) Project 2.A.1 Evaluate System Control Improvements.

The purpose indicated on page 4-2.11 was to "ensure that the database balances to the General Ledger." As this user requirement was not pursued, more waste was created.

Page 4-2.13 stipulated that "History to Database balancing requirements will be addressed as part of Project 4.A.1, Online Borrower History Inquiry." This requirement was not pursued.

And on Page 4-2.12 of Project 2-A-1, "Database Architecture ...assure the database structure compliments the FmHA organizational structure to assure the database structure will support current and future requirements." There was no Conceptual nor General Design of the SFSI system and no pursuit of this requirement. Further, there was more waste as management did not investigate my computer processing control Employee Suggestions #78 "GUARD AGAINST COMPUTER HACKERS" and FC-301 "PROVIDE BETTER AUDIT TRAIL."

d) With inadequate planning and the absence of a computer Conceptual and General Design, all SFSI project subsystems failed to meet user requirements and expectations.

e) A Conceptual/general Design for SFSI by Windisch suggestion FC-504 "DESIGN AND IMPLEMENT ALSIS" was rejected.

Congress was not notified of the dismal failure of "SFSI."

5. ORACLE Database Implementation (ODI)

After the failure of the SPSI project, the Information Resources Management administrator blindly purchased the ORACLE Database System, and reorganized Automated Information Services (AIS) into two separate divisions.

a) There were no plans nor General Design for the use of the ORACLE Database System.
b) An existing IDMS Database System could be developed to provide an efficient Online Loan Servicing System.
c) There was no cost/benefit analysis on the feasibility of developing either the ORACLE or the IDMS Database Systems.
d) Separating AIS into two separate divisions was contrary to the development of efficient integrated systems.

With this additional evidence, I resubmitted my Employee Suggestion FC-523 "REORGANIZE AIS" on July 13, 1990. There was no discussion nor investigation of my suggestion.

On August 11, 1990, I wrote to Congressman Gephardt about my concerns, including, "A recent reorganization of Automated Information Services does not make the necessary changes involving computer system design responsibility; therefore, I have resubmitted my Employee Suggestion for Reorganization."

During continuing correspondence with Congressman Gephardt, on December 21, 1990, I pointed out, "it is likely that the purchase of ORACLE, (another database, costing $21,000,000) may well be a total waste of the taxpayers money."

Gephardt's office showed no interest in my concerns, and did not take my concerns to the Agriculture committee. I was told to contact the committee on my own.

On July 16, 1991, I sent my "CRITICAL REPORT" to Congressman Kika de la Garza, the Chairman of the Agriculture Committee for the House of Representatives. I volunteered to testify at a pending hearing. There was *no investigation* of my report, and my offer to testify was rejected.

In October 1991, the House Agriculture Subcommittee, chaired by congressman Glenn English, issued a General Accounting Office report GAO/

I,TEC-92-9, titled, "ADP MODERNIZATION Half-Billion Dollar FmHA effort.Lacks Adequate Planning and Oversight."

The ORACLE database system was purchased without any idea nor "General Design" for its use. And user requirements for confidentially and data processing controls, which are well documented by the failed Automated Program Delivery System (APDS), were not even considered.

A Windisch suggestion FC-504 "DESIGN AND IMPLEMENT ALSIS" showing a computer "General Design" for using the IDMS system was ignored.

In my Whistleblower Complaint, I showed the wasteful purchase of the ORACLE system by using a Cost Analysis chart, dated December 18, 1990. This chart compares nineteen items of cost using the IDMS system, against the cost of using the ORACLE system. ORACLE had sixteen items with greater cost than IDMS, and ORACLE had three items with the cost equal to IDMS. ORACLE had *zero* items with lesser cost than IDMS.

Results of Implementation of ORACLE

According to an article in the January 15, 1996 *U.S. News and World Report*: "The Farmers Home Administration manages its loan portfolio with color-coded index cards, despite spending $200 million on computer systems to perform the task."

A half-billion dollars has been wasted and county office work has doubled and failure after failure after failure after failure continues.

CHAPTER SIX
QUESTIONABLE CONTROLS WITH ORACLE

Computer giant IBM designed the original structured data base systems which are used in today's design of complex integrated computer systems.

The first such system was a top to bottom pyramid structure known as a Bill Of Materials (BOM) database, which was used primarily in the manufacturing industry for production and inventory control. This BOM database system was also used successfully in the design of financial and other types of computer management systems.

IBM also developed a second database system which has a bottom to top pyramid structure, know as a Relational database because of the relational location of data elements within the computer file. A Relational type database system is easier to understand and very easy to implement. But in my learned experience, the Relational type database was found to be very inefficient, and its bottom to top structure does not allow for the design of top down controls which are possible by using the BOM database system.

In 1982, the Department of Agriculture purchased and leased the Integrated Database Management System (IDMS), which is an improved BOM system. After many failures to develop integrated IDMS systems, the administrator for Information Resources Management purchased ORACLE, a Relational database system, as a means to provide the thousands of field offices with computer loan servicing.

The ORACLE Database System was purchased without any idea nor "General Design" for its use. And user requirements for confidentially and data processing controls, which are well documented in the design of the Automated Program Delivery System (APDS), were not considered.

Windisch showed how the IDMS Database System can and should be used by presenting a computer "General Design" in his suggestion FC-504 "DESIGN AND IMPLEMENT ALSIS."

Data Processing Controls

The design of the APDS system using an IDMS database shows how policy and procedures can be dictated at the top level in the National office, and with maximum controls loan information can be sent down to, and retrieved from, the bottom levels of field, district, and state offices.

Conversely, the ORACLE Database System is featured as an open system allowing easy access to information; a system that defies efforts to establish adequate data processing controls.

Observe an advertisement in Federal Computer Week on December 5, 1994: "GATEWAYS NOW OPEN 24 hours a day, 7 days a week. Access all of your information—wherever it resides--on personal digital assistants, PCs, workstations, minis, mainframes, or scalable parallel systems. We remove all the boundaries between you and your information for instant access anywhere anytime. Our ORACLE database and tools allows you to access, integrate, and update from anywhere on the network."

Furthermore, the ORACLE Corporation brags that their computer instruction programs can operate or perform successfully on all platforms or levels of computers from mini-computers to mainframe-computers. This universal compatibility also allows any computer program to be modified at any of the multiple locations where the ORACLE system resides. This flexibility challenges any security system to guard against fraudulent modification of computer programs.

At Agriculture, the ORACLE system which has a bottom to top organization, allows each of the thousands of field servicing offices to create and maintain their own independent computer loan files, and allows any individual office to share their computer files with any other office in the system. Bottom to top system architecture provides for individual field office computer files to be electronically exported to a district office where the files are combined to create a district file. The district files are then exported to the state office to create a state file; and the state files are exported to the national office to create a national computer loan file.

With easy access to computer files between field offices, there is little or no control by the national office over what happens at or between the individual field offices. While state and district offices can look at any office files to monitor what happens at individual field offices, there are no automatic internal computer controls to detect nor stop unwarranted tampering with data.

Field office managers have rightfully questioned the need to update and maintain two computer loan files, their own ORACLE field office file plus the national Program Loan Accounting System (PLAS) file. It is natural for field office managers to keep a third file of color-coded index cards, in case they must prove which set of computer files is correct.

Agriculture's financial management has resisted further implementation and use of ORACLE as the basic loan servicing system. Financial management has not permitted the updating of loan payments to the field office files as a means to eliminate the national PLAS file update. Without updating of the PLAS national files, there will be no controls of field office activity, and there will be no national balancing of bank deposits to an updated loan file.

A 1991 issue of *Government Computer News* raised questions. "Vendors of database management systems are concerned about the way a database security standard is being developed. The NSA's National Computer Security Center (NCSC) has been working on its Trusted Database Interpretation for more than a year with the help of ORACLE Corp., but the contract to help develop a draft standard was made public only recently."

If you believe the General Accounting Office (GAO) reports about the state of computer security in federal agencies, it is clear no one is in charge on a national level. When Clifford Stoll was on the tracks of the West German hacker, he could not find anyone at either National Institute of Standards and Technology (NIST) or National Security Agency (NSA), who was willing to help him alert federal agencies whose computers were under attack.

Inefficient Computer System

In my Whistleblower Complaint, I reported the wasteful purchase of the ORACLE system. My Cost Analysis chart dated December 18, 1990, compares nineteen items of cost using the IDMS system, against the cost of using the ORACLE system. ORACLE had sixteen items with greater cost than IDMS, and three items with ORACLE cost equal to IDMS. ORACLE had zero items with lesser cost than the IDMS system.

The most notable and drastic difference in costs between the two systems are shown in line items 1.b. and 3.b. Item 1.b. shows that the IDMS software system requires a purchase/lease for four area computer centers, while the ORACLE software system requires a purchase/lease for 2500 county offices. And item 3.b. shows that there are ongoing System Operating Costs for the IDMS system at four area computer sites, while ORACLE incurs ongoing System Operating Costs at 2500 county offices.

Continued Use of Oracle Increases Continuing Waste

The continued use of ORACLE to develop independent computer systems *increases* the ongoing waste of current inefficient computer systems. In addition each newly implemented inefficient system will increase the task of redesign and will postpone the urgently needed implementation of reliable computer systems and controls at Agriculture.

Reorganization of Agriculture Fails

In 1992, I wrote many letters to Senator Richard G. Lugar, a member of the Senate Agriculture committee. Senator Lugar was working on a plan to reorganize the Department of Agriculture. I asked Senator Lugar to investigate my Whistleblower Complaint with Agriculture, to show that Information Resource Management (IRM) must be reorganized first, to have a successful reorganization of Agriculture. Senator Lugar sent me an article about his reorganization plans, but there was no investigation of my Complaint and suggestion.

In October 1996, Senator Lugar sent me a copy of a new bill titled "The Department of Agriculture Responsibility and Accountability Act of 1996," and he planned to introduce the bill again in the l05th Congress of 1997.

Senator Lugar's statement regarding the need for this new bill included, "The General Accounting Office, the Department of Agriculture's Office of Inspector General, and independent contractor reviews since 1989 have identified ongoing problems with UDSA's administration of information resource management programs, including the multiagency program called Info Share and computer and telecommunication purchases. Since the USDA Reorganization Act was enacted in 1994, USDA management has continued their historic trend of purchasing telecommunication and information systems that: fail to link information technology budgeting and purchases to strategic business needs; fail to integrate information management strategies with financial and programmatic information and reporting requirements; fail to define information technology requirements through business process reengineering; fail to achieve department-wide efficiencies by standardizing administrative functions; and, fail to address the cultural changes necessary to migrate from a piecemeal approach to a standardized, collaborative delivery system in Field Service Centers.

> The Department continues to acquire hardware, software and other equipment that does not match user needs, provides inefficient delivery of services to USDA customers, and creates unnecessary duplication. Many duplicated product and service acquisitions could have been avoided by department wide consolidation and sharing. Procurement activities do not allow the Farm Services Agency, Natural Resources Conservation Service and Rural Development to exchange information electronically in the agency headquarter and field offices. The Department lacks leadership to direct the changes necessary to establish a working Field Service Center infrastructure.

In an October 7, 1996 letter to Senator Lugar, I wrote, "I applaud your continuing efforts to correct the failure of the Information Revolution at Agriculture. Furthermore, if you combine your efforts with my suggestion to "Reorganize Information Resources Management," you will help correct the GOVERNMENT-WIDE failure of the Information Revolution and our country's financial management Crisis.'"

On February 22, 1997, I wrote to Senator Lugar and sent copies to sixty other senators. "Your work at Agriculture will provide the solutions for our government's FINANCIAL MANAGEMENT CRISIS.

> You must use your jurisdiction to bypass the incompetent Office of Special Counsel (attached), and reinvestigate my 1991 Whistleblower (WB) Complaint about GROSS WASTE AND GROSS MISMANAGEMENT of Information Resources and Technology.

On March 19, 1997 I wrote to these same Senators, "I beg and urge your prompt attention to our nation's serious financial management crisis, which I have summarized in the attached letter to President Clinton.

> This financial crisis will NOT go away. It will only get worse as Unreliable Controls increase Chaotic Accounting, and the mysteries of unreliable computer systems continue to confuse and frustrate financial management and the Inspector Generals (OIG). And without the Computer Professional in government, there is nobody to design efficient and reliable computer systems.
> The design and implementation of reliable computer systems and controls will not be an easy task. And some *will* say it's impossible to correct such a massive government-wide mess.
> Again I plead and beg that YOU, as a member of the Senate, take immediate steps for corrective action.

On March 27, 1997, I faxed the following to Senator Lugar. "An employee at USDA recently wrote to me that the ORACLE System is still being promoted for use in the design of new stand-alone computer systems which are inefficient. Stand alone systems that will cause further problems for fiscal management."

From my March 19, 1997 request for help from sixty Senators, I received six acknowledgments, with no offers to help, and several courtesy referrals to my own Senator.

Since 1994, I have sent many letters to my Missouri Senator John Ashcroft, requesting that he meet with me and my advisors to discuss this serious financial management crisis.

Senator Ashcroft's only answer to numerous requests came in a July 19, 1996 letter from Amy Brocklage White, the St. Louis District Office Director. *In my opinion this letter shows that Senator Ashcroft does not believe and/or does not understand that there is a financial management crisis.*

The July 19, 1996 letter states: "Dear Mr. Windisch, Thank you for your correspondence to Senator Ashcroft on April 25 and June 26, 1996. The Senator has asked that I respond directly to you. As you know, I thoroughly reviewed the documentation you submitted as well as your proposed solutions following our meeting in the district office.

Unfortunately, based on our research, both the nature of these computer problems and the appropriateness of your solutions have changed significantly in the past several years. New systems have provided a very real opportunity to address the problems of the past.

. As you are aware, recent House legislation was proposed and passed to address the very issues of waste and poor management systems you highlight. It is my belief that this legislation reflects your concerns for all government agencies.

In addition, conversations with the Department of Labor have clarified that you do not fit the criteria established for a federal Whistleblower. If you wish to pursue a Whistleblower complaint, I suggest you reopen your case with the Office of Special Counsel in Washington, D.C.

As technology continues to revolutionize the way Washington does business, Senator Ashcroft believes our government bureaucracy will be called to a new standard of organization and accountability. I know this is your wish as well.

Thank you for sharing your insights with us.

After additional letters I learned that my correspondence was filed away in Senator Ashcroft's Office of Constituent Services at Jefferson City, while I live in St. Louis where the Agriculture Department office is located.

CHAPTER SEVEN
COMPUTER PAPERWORK VS. MANUAL PAPERWORK

While the Paperwork Reduction Act and the Information Revolution may have reduced manual paperwork, it also has greatly increased the amount of automatically generated computer reports. Since 1980, Congress continues to receive bigger and better computer reports. It is no wonder that congressional staffs have doubled in order to review and manually sort through these mountains of computer reports.

When Senator Richard Lugar announced that Agriculture was being reorganized, I again wrote to him. I asked that he review my report "Government Computers Add To Waste," and I suggested that Information Resources Management must be reorganized in conjunction with his reorganization plans.

Senator Lugar did not investigate my story, but he did send me a copy of a magazine article explaining how the Department of Agriculture was being reorganized. This article featured a picture of Senator Lugar and Chuck Conner, staff director, standing in front of stacks of computer reports that were two to three feet high. It is said a picture is worth a thousand words.

I demonstrated this very problem about inefficient computer reports causing more waste. Farmers Home Administration, USDA, had a computerized Deposit Fund system which was designed to match loan payments against loan account updates, and print a report of unmatched payments and updates. It required seven to eight weeks to manually reconcile this two foot stack of the monthly Deposit Fund Balance List.

As a computer professional, I drafted a Process Flow Chart, analyzed each step of the process, and designed an Online Deposit Fund system. The new system automated seventeen of the original twenty-eight manual work tasks, and the reconciling of a monthly Deposit Fund Balance List is now completed in one to two weeks.

This reduction of manual effort from eight weeks to two weeks shows that an unbelievable 75 percent more manual work had been built into the original design of this computerized Deposit Fund system.

CHAPTER EIGHT
GOVERNMENT BUREAUCRACY

**'The Government May Not Be Falling, But Big Chunks
Of It Sure Are Crashing Down'**

Corrective Administration Action

Throughout my nine years working for Farmers Home Administration, USDA, I worked diligently and hard to achieve a successful implementation of the information revolution. Failing to solve the problems of computer automation by example and professional work ethic, I then tried every known and learned administrative procedure in order to bring attention to these serious problems.

I was hired by FmHA as a computer Programmer Analyst, GS-334-11, in November, 1982. In December, 1983, I applied for the position of Systems Account, GS-510-12, a position with responsibility for the design of Automated Data Processing (ADP) computer systems. Having a nationally recognized professional CDP certification, plus ten years past experience as Manager of Computer Systems Design, I believed I was more than qualified for this position of Systems Accountant.

My application was rejected, and also my documented qualifications appeal for FmHA certification to be recognized as being qualified for this position, was also rejected.

Despite this official rejection for promotion into a position of computer systems design, in October 1984, I was detailed to review the computer systems design aspects of the Accounting Program Delivery System (APDS), which was designed by Price Waterhouse. This responsibility was very similar to my previous position as Manager of Computer Systems Design! This assignment of monitoring APDS design lasted through the end of 1985.

I made a number of valuable suggestions to enhance the design of the new APDS system, which consisted of nineteen subsystems and twenty-one Volumes (approximately forty books) of documentation. Most notable was my review and presentation of the computer Processing Controls sub-system.

On November 14, 1985, a Price Waterhouse representative contacted me for a walk-through and a review of the Processing Control problems, and I pointed out the absence of financial control totals on the computer loan file.

On November 20, 1985, I was notified that Price Waterhouse was rewriting Program AOBR200 specifications and they were adding the BALHEAD and BALDTL control records in order to provide for generation of automatic computer audits.

After 1985, while working as a computer Programmer Analyst, I made numerous informal ADP design suggestions, and I was told that design was not part of my job nor responsibility. Because of this directive, I was entitled to and did submit over two dozen Employee Suggestions involving the design of ADP systems.

By 1987, I became aware of the tremendous waste of computer resources at FmHA, and most alarming, was my discovery of the absence of ADP financial controls at FmHA. In 1987 I first submitted my Employee Suggestion to reorganize ADP so that the accountants would be replaced by professional computer Systems Analysts who would then be responsible for Work Analysis, Cost Justification, and finally, the design of ADP systems and ADP controls.

Government managers have always contended that federal computer professionals were not needed in government, because government can always hire outside contractors like Price Waterhouse to design computer systems for the government. But in 1987, the Accounting Program Delivery System (APDS) which was expertly designed by Price Waterhouse, was in shambles and never implemented.

The General Accounting Office (GAO) reported that this APDS system failed because of the following reasons. 1.) Price Waterhouse did not complete the system design. 2.) Programming contractor did not meet contract obligations. 3.) Government contract administrator failed to expedite job.

GAO Was Wrong on All Three Counts.

1. The design of a large computer system is a dynamic ongoing design development task, which is not completed until the last computer program is written and implemented. The Price Waterhouse contract was terminated after OAO the programming contractor came onto the job, and Price Waterhouse had no further responsibility for ongoing design development. Price Waterhouse was unjustly accused.

2. The programming contractor, who was not responsible for ongoing design development, had some serious design questions. But the federal Systems Accountant supervisor did not understand the design questions and had no answers. And the programming contractor was wrongly sued for failure to meet contract obligations,

3. The government contract administrator may have been confused, but he was also wrongfully faulted.

Executive Order Has Failed

President Clinton issued an executive order to reinvent government.
On March 26, 1993, I sent my report about "Government Computers Add To Waste" with the following cover letter to President Clinton.

"Please classify my story as a NATIONAL EMERGENCY.

"I claim that with INADEQUATE COMPUTER CONTROLS, IMPOSSIBLE AUDITS, AND CHAOTIC ACCOUNTING, NOBODY KNOWS THE TRUE FINANCIAL CONDITION OF OUR COUNTRY.

"IF FOREIGN COUNTRIES ARE NOW CAUTIOUS ABOUT INVESTING IN OUR NATIONAL DEBT, WHAT WILL MY STORY DO TO THEIR CONFIDENCE?"

"For 6 years, neither Congress nor the highest government officials have dared to investigate."

I wrote several follow up letters, and finally received the following letter on August 12, 1993;

> President Clinton has forwarded your letter of May 25, 1993, to the General Services Administration for review and response. We appreciate your observations regarding management and control of information systems throughout the Federal government.
>
> As an organization having oversight responsibility regarding Federal information processing resources, we are extremely concerned with the quality and security of information maintained by the Federal government. Contributions from concerned citizens provide valuable input to our review and regulatory programs helping us to identify areas where acquisition, development and use of Federal information systems could be improved. This type of contribution is particularly critical for our efforts to reinventing government, so that, effective management of government accounting can be accomplished.
>
> Again, our sincere thanks for the information you have provided.

There was no further correspondence, and *no investigation.*

On November 11, 1993, I sent my report to Secretary of Treasury Lloyd Bentsen advising him of my concerns about Inadequate Controls. In my letter I asked,

> ...In the absence of a new Inspector General for USDA. I call on you as the nation's Chief Fiscal Officer to command an immediate investigation of USDA, so that you can take prompt corrective action to eliminate this chaotic and scandalous fiscal coverup.

On March 3, 1994, I sent a follow up letter to Secretary Bentsen which included the following statements,

> A recent request by the banking committee for the GAO to investigate the audit procedures of the Federal Reserve tells me that you do not understand the serious urgency of my request for a meeting.
>
> In my past dealings with the Federal Reserve, I found that the Federal Reserve was the one government agency that has effectively

used computer automation and understands the use of computer Internal Controls. This audit request is like a first grader (GAO) reviewing the work of a teacher (Federal Reserve).

My request will also effect your thinking about plans to reorganize and consolidate the four existing banking and monetary control agencies. The country has everything to gain by merging the three agencies that don't work. But also merging the Federal Reserve and disrupting its important monetary control policies may not be such a good idea. In addition, a single monetary control agency with top down autocratic management will be highly susceptible to collusion.

On March 24, 1994, I received the following letter from Jane L. Sullivan Director, Office of Information Resources Management of the Department of Treasury,

> In response to your letter of March 3, 1994, I am forwarding it to the Treasury Reinvention Team of the National Performance Review. I believe that the Reinvention Team will objectively evaluate your observations in the interest of a more efficient and effective government process.
>
> I appreciate the views expressed in your letter over the need for Computer Internal Controls, an issue that is of concern throughout the Federal Government.

There was *no investigation.*

Vice President Al Gore heads the panel to cut waste and "Reinvent Government." Al Gore said that efficiency recommendations by the Grace Commission were seen as "adversarial" because it was a private commission nosing around among public workers. He said President Clinton wants to get federal employees involved in the review.

I sent my report about "Government Computers Add To Waste" to Vice President Gore, which was answered July 29, 1993.

> Thank you for writing to me about "reinventing government" and the work of the National Performance Review. I appreciate having the benefit of your views and suggestions concerning our government, how it works, and how it can be improved.
>
> I am encouraged by the overwhelming response for this effort from citizens across America in both the public and private sectors. Many of the very best ideas about improving government and eliminating waste are coming from citizens who have a strong desire to make our government more effective, more efficient and more responsive. You are providing valuable information, not only about

solving problems that have been well documented and publicized, but also about problems that might otherwise have gone unnoticed.

Please be assured that each and every letter received is being studied closely, and your ideas will be considered carefully as an essential part of our work. I welcome your participation in the National Performance Review, and I hope you will continue to take an active role in the effort to improve government.

There was *no investigation.*

Because management looks at employee suggestions as mere criticism of the way they are running the government, federal employees are told to take their complaints about waste and theft to their agency Office of Inspector General, which has a history of protecting their fellow agency managers.

Many federal employees have gone further and filed complaints under the Whistleblower Protection Act. In 1993, GAO reported that 78 percent of the 662 federal Whistleblowers that they surveyed, believed their complaints were *not adequately investigated.*

The President's Executive Order to "Reinvent Government" will fail because the ideas of federal employees are ignored.

IRM Bureaucracy Reinvents Computer Waste

The Paperwork Reduction Act of 1980 formally established Information Resources Management (IRM) within the Federal Government. This Act introduced the principle of information as a strategic resource that has value and costs. It also promoted the use of information technology such as computers and telecommunications to improve the collection, use, and dissemination of information by federal agencies.

Since 1980, the U.S. General Accounting Office (GAO) has continually reported about computer automation failures throughout the federal government. And in my article "Government Computers Add To Waste," which appeared in the *St. Louis Post-Dispatch* in 1993, I estimated that more than a *half-trillion dollars* has already been lost on inefficient and sometimes useless computer automation.

In 1993, I wrote to President Bill Clinton about the gross mismanagement of IRM. I referred to my Whistleblower Complaint, and I stated, "...the 'Chief Financial Officers Act' cannot succeed until Computer Automation is REORGANIZED."

In my Complaint, I recommended that Computer Automation must be reorganized. I explained that planning for an integrated computer system is similar to planning for integrated housing such as a hotel, and there must be a General Design. My documentation showed that Federal IRM does not use a General Design when planning Integrated Computer Systems.

President Clinton referred my complaint to the U.S. General Services

Administration (GSA), and GSA *did not investigate*. In December of 1993, GSA issued a new "Information Resources Management Strategic Planning Guide" called FEDSIM.

On the first page of FEDSIM, under executive summary, is a question, "Would you give a contractor $500,000 to build a house for you lacking a house plan and proof that the job can be done?"

FEDSIM shows no General Design plan for an integrated housing hotel. We do not know if the $500,000 floor plan will be located on the top floor, or located on the first floor of the hotel. And where is the General Design as "...proof that the job can be done?"

As in the past, GSA'S FEDSIM gives no creditable guidance about planning for integrated computer systems.

I requested an investigation of IRM mismanagement from Senator Sam Nunn, Chairman of the Permanent Subcommittee on Investigations. Subcommittee Chief Counsel, Eleanor J. Hill, answered my request,

> ...Your concern is not misplaced. Congress's audit arm, the General Accounting Office, has reported about these and other problems in the Government's computer systems. The GAO is working with the Office of Management and Budget, the General Services Administration, the Department of Commerce's National Institute of Standards and Technology (all which formulate policies, procedures, and standards to monitor individual agency information resource management activities), and all the individual federal agencies to identify weaknesses and develop solutions. Substantial issue areas remain; however, the GAO reports progress is being made.
>
> You might consider contacting the GAO directly about your concern and your ideas for reinventing this area of government planning and acquisition. I would direct you to Mr. Jack L. Brock, who handles financial and information management issues at the GAO....

I contacted Mr. Brock of GAO, and he sent me a copy of GAO'S testimony before a Committee on Governmental Affairs, United States Senate, on May 19, 1994. This testimony was about the reauthorization of the Paperwork Reduction Act.

Throughout the report GAO cites problem after problem with IRM's computer automation and states:

> GAO's work has clearly shown that federal agencies have great difficulty in effectively managing technology... spends over $25 billion annually...does not get adequate return on investment." GAO does not identify any area's of IRM mismanagement, and they do not offer any solutions to the barrage of problems.

Responsibility and oversight is claimed in part by IRM Managers, Office of Management and Budget (OMB), Chief Financial Officer (CFO), General Services Administration (GSA), General Accounting Office (GAO), National Institute of Standards and Technology (NIST), and the National Security Agency (NSA). There is no central responsibility for Information Resources Management.

In addition, oversight by the agencies Office of Inspector General (OIG), and the 1989 Whistleblower Protection Act, have been extremely ineffective.

I sent my reports and suggestions for modifying the Paperwork Reduction Act to the Senate Governmental Affairs committee. *There was no investigation.*

Congress passed the 1995 Paperwork Reduction Act without correcting the problems of mismanagement of Information Resources. This means we will have four more years of continued computer waste, unreliable financial controls, and more chaotic financial accounting.

Oversight Responsibility

1. President and Congress

The Clinton administration is in awe of cyberspace and the information superhighway, while Gingrich and Congress struggle with their Howdy Doody system of Internet and E-mail, but they all have closed their eyes and ears to these serious financial management issues.

2. Office of Management and Budget (OMB)

Because OMB is most dependent on receiving reliable financial information from all other government agencies and departments, OMB was given primary oversight responsibility for government-wide Information Resources Management (IRM), under the Paperwork Reduction Act (PRA).

In a futile effort to address government's serious financial management issues, Congress through the PRA of 1995, has thrown more money into OMB's oversight budget.

It is impractical to expect OMB to oversee and/or correct the entire universe of government's Information Resources Management problems.

OMB should only be responsible for its Information Resources Management within OMB. And OMB must demand that it receive timely and reliable financial data from all other government departments.

In data processing language, GI/GO means Garbage In / Garbage Out. This saying warns that unreliable financial data from other government departments can only produce unreliable OMB financial reports.

3. General Accounting Office (GAO)

GAO gives fair warning in its report "Financial Management Issues." And GAO has diligently reported continuing failures of computer automation projects.

Off the record, GAO admits that they have few experts in the field of Information Resources Management.

4. General Services Administration (GSA)

The GSA Administrator is referred to as the "Computer Czar" because each year his department brokers the purchase of computers and information technology worth billions of dollars.

GSA believes the information revolution is successful, because of the government wide use of personal computers (PCs), laptop computers (LTs), telecommunication systems, and standard plug-in office management systems such as WordPerfect, Scheduling, and Lotus 1-2-3.

Beyond PCs and standard office management systems, GSA does not seem to understand the serious problems of inefficient mainframe computers with its unreliable systems and controls.

During the purchase of expensive information technology, vendors often use subtle methods to promote their products.

While working in the private sector, I saw vendors offer important officials and spouses a week long seminar at a resort. Two hours a day were spent on product presentation, and the rest of the day was socializing and recreation.

GSA should only be responsible for Information Resources Management within GSA. And GSA should be relieved of all IRM responsibility for all other agencies and departments.

5. National Institute of Standards and Technology (NIST) and National Security Agency (NSA)

Congress was uncomfortable with computer security responsibility resting with NSA, and as part of the 1987 Computer Security Act, placed NIST in the lead role. NSA is supposed to act in an advisory capacity.

If you believe the General Accounting Office (GAO) reports about the state of computer security in federal agencies, it is clear no one is in charge.

When Clifford Stoll was on the tracks of the West German hacker, he could not find anyone at either NIST or NSA who was willing to help him alert federal agencies whose computers were under attack.

Neither agency understands the GAO report of "Financial Management Issues." They do not realize that government wide unreliable financial controls means that many agencies having unreliable controls cannot be aware of a hacker attack, and *cannot know if money is missing!*

There was a puzzling story in *Government Computer News*, "Vendors of data base management systems are concerned about the way a data base security standard is being developed. The National Security Agency's (NSA) National Computer Security Center (NCSC) has been working on its Trusted Database Interpretation for more than a year with the help of Oracle Corp., but the contract to help develop a draft standard was made public only recently."

In its quest for access security, it is strange that NSA would favor the ORACLE data base system, a data base system advertised as an open system, an Open System that defies the development of computer access security.

The following is an advertisement from *Federal Computer Week*, December 5, 1994 edition:

GATEWAYS NOW OPEN
24 hours a day, 7 days a week.
Access all of your information--wherever
it resides--on personal digital assistants,
PCs, workstations, minis, mainframes, or
scalable parallel systems.
We remove all the boundaries between you and your
information for instant access anywhere, anytime.
ORACLE GOVERNMENT

It is evident, no one is in charge of computer security.

6. Office of Technology Assessment (OTA)

OTA is working on information security and privacy in network environments. Areas of interest are safeguarding networked information, legal issues and information security, and government policies and cryptographic safeguards. Responsibilities of OTA do not include computer security.

7. Office of Special Counsel (OSC) See Whistleblower Protection Act a Waste in Chapter Ten.

8. Office of Inspector General (OIG)

The president appoints an Inspector General for each government agency to be a guardian against waste and fraud.

I made numerous calls and wrote many letters about computer waste and unreliable financial controls to the Office of Inspector General (OIG) at Agriculture. My telephone calls were either not returned, or not returned promptly. And most of my numerous correspondence was not even acknowledged and *not investigated.*

Furthermore, government regulations recommend that Inspector Generals and Chief Financial Officers should have professional qualifications for their job positions. I recommend that,

If every publicly held corporation is required to have its financial statements examined by a certified public accounting firm; then the citizen stock holders of our country are entitled to require each Inspector General and each Chief Financial Officer to maintain professional CPA certification.

9. Information Resources Management (IRM)

The IRM administrator must be held accountable for the success or failure for all management of Information Resources within the administrator's department.

IRM must be reorganized so that certified computer professionals are in charge of designing efficient and reliable computer systems and controls.

IRM cannot blame failures of computer automation on to the users because they either ask for too little automation or often ask for the impossible. IRM needs to perform a professional process flow analysis, construct efficient process steps, reconcile user requirement differences, provide a General Design, and provide a cost/benefit analysis. It is IRM's job to design efficient and reliable computer systems and controls.

A supervisor of IRM at Agriculture received national honors from the Association of Government Accountants (AGA) for adopting Life Cycle Methodology (LCM) procedures for designing computer systems. My Whistleblower Complaint shows that the critical LCM process tasks of Conceptual Design, and General Design were not being performed. This is confirmed by the agency's own Project Life Cycle chart of June 1990.

The problems of federal Information Resources Management (IRM) are so bad, that Robert V. Head retold an old story from the 1960s, which appeared in *Government Computer News* on December 8, 1991.

> There is an old story concerning three letters left behind by an IRM manager who had just been fired. He advised his successor to open the first of the letters in case of trouble on the job and to open the remaining ones if his troubles recurred.
>
> The first letter contained the message, 'Blame your problems on your predecessor.' The second instructed the manager, 'Reorganize your department.' And the third directed the by now beleaguered manager to 'Sit down and write three letters.'

That is exactly what happened at the Department of Agriculture. Mark Boster was hired as the new Assistant Administrator responsible for managing IRM. In 1991, in front of a House Agriculture committee, Mark Boster blamed prior IRM problems on his predecessor Roger Cooper. Then Mark Boster reorganized his IRM department. And when his troubles recurred, Mark Boster resigned. I guess he sat down and wrote three letters.

Meanwhile, Roger Cooper who was blamed for the prior problems of IRM at Agriculture, had resigned to work for the Justice Department as the new deputy assistant attorney general for IRM.

Here is part of the story that appeared in the *Government Computer News* on April 1, 1991.

> As Justice's first designated IRM chief, Cooper will oversee the department's computer services, telecommunications services, legal and information systems, and systems policy staffs. Major projects under way at Justice include the office automation effort, Project Eagle, and a department wide case management procurement."
> Cooper comes to Justice at a time of strife. The department's IRM reorganization last fall coincided with the release of a General

Accounting Office report recommending that Justice strengthen its IRM structure.

In 1995, Roger Cooper, who was instrumental in the purchase of the failed ORACLE/I-NET system at the Department of Agriculture, left the Justice Department to work as a vice president at I-NET Inc. Was this pay back time?

Paul Light in his book about the federal work force wrote, "The big problem with managers managing managers is that no one is accountable for what goes right or wrong."

CHAPTER NINE
CORRECTIVE LEGISLATIVE ACTION

Since 1990, I have diligently pursued every known and learned legislative action to have these serious problems addressed and corrected.

I have written and appealed to both presidents Bush and Clinton to investigate my Whistleblower Complaint, and both rejected my plea. Hundreds of letters were sent to cabinet members of both presidential administrations, and to dozens of congressional representatives. Most of my correspondence went unanswered. I received some courteous form letters, usually as follows,

"Thank you for your important letter. It is letters from concerned citizens like you that help make our country great. Thanks for your continued support. And please continue to share with me, your thoughts and concerns. Sincerely," *but no investigation.*

Only two or three congressional members like Senators Glenn and Lugar seemed interested. They seemed to have genuine concerns about computer fraud and waste, but they did not take the time to investigate.

Several years ago, I communicated extensively with Senator John Glenn and his staff on the Senate Governmental Affairs Committee. I wrote that the problem of breaking computer security at IRS, as discovered by government auditors, was compounded by government wide unreliable computer Internal Controls. I pointed out that the IRS Rapid Refund Scam and the fraudulent Earned Income Tax Credit returns occur because of unreliable computer Internal Controls. And nobody can know how much money is being stolen by these and other fraudulent schemes.

In response I was informed that Senator Glenn was co-sponsor of the 1990 Chief Financial Officer Act, which establishes financial responsibility to assure adequate controls and reliable financial reporting, and that Congress had awarded $8 billion for new IRS computer systems.

In 1995, the IRS came out with their first major system change. The computer was used to cross-check the spelling of names on income tax returns with the name/s as recorded on IRS computers. Millions of honest tax payers were angry and frustrated because their tax returns were bounced around for months before their returns could be reconciled. This is a poor way to establish computer Internal Controls.

Then I worked for almost a year trying to have the Senate Governmental Affairs committee investigate my report and recommendations for amending the new Paperwork Reduction Act. The committee *did not investigate my report* nor my solutions. The new Paperwork Reduction Act of 1995 only throws more money at the problem, and modifies the Brooks Act to satisfy government's vendors of Electronic Technology.

On September 14, 1993, I wrote the following to Senator Glenn,

Re: COMPUTER FIASCO - CHAOTIC ACCOUNTING

1. The PAPERWORK REDUCTION ACT has created a FEDERAL FIASCO OF COMPUTER AUTOMATION, causing GROSS MISMANAGEMENT & GROSS WASTE.

2. The EMPLOYEE SUGGESTION PLAN (ESP) giving federal employees a voice to eliminate waste, DOES NOT WORK.

3. The WHISTLE BLOWER PROTECTION ACT OF 1989, DOES NOT WORK.

4. The INSPECTOR GENERAL ACT OF 1978, DOES NOT WORK.
   a. The USDA Inspector General under Bush was inept.
   b. A new Inspector General (IG) for USDA is not yet selected.
   c. Senate must insist that IG be a CPA accountant.

5. The CHIEF FINANCIAL OFFICER ACT OF 1990 has done NOTHING TO CORRECT THE PROBLEMS of irresponsible CHAOTIC ACCOUNTING.
WHEN ARE YOU AND CONGRESS GOING TO BEGIN INVESTIGATING MY EVIDENCE AND STORY TO END CHAOTIC GOVERNMENT ACCOUNTING AND STOP THE THEFT OF BILLIONS OF OUR TAX DOLLARS?"

There was *no investigation*.

While getting the run around by committees, Congress, and the establishment; I also sent hundreds of letters to my *own* congressman, Richard A. Gephardt.

My Congressional Representative

I spent over five years, sent more than one-thousand pages of correspondence, and made more than one-hundred telephone calls to my congressman Richard A. Gephardt. And still he refuses to represent me. He will not meet with me, and he refuses to investigate my Whistleblower Complaint about government's massive waste and theft.

On August 11, 1990, I began writing to my congressman,

Be advised, that there is NO INTERNAL CONTROL of the computer database for the 57 billion dollar loan portfolio administered by Farmers Home Administration (FmHA), and without internal controls it is unknown how much money is lost through computer theft and/or computer processing.
There was no investigation.

In December 1990, I informed Congressman Gephardt that there had been no meetings about my complaints and/or suggestions. In this same letter I advised,

...it is likely that the purchase of ORACLE, (another database costing $21,000,000) may well be a total waste of the taxpayers money."
There was no investigation.

A May 1, 1991 letter informed Congressman Gephardt, after one meeting with the Deputy Assistant Administrator for Financial Systems (ADP), Edward R. Ates, that this is what happened,

I understand that Mr. Ates questioned his boss, Mr. Mark Boster, the Assistant Administrator for Financial Systems, about the purchase of the expensive ORACLE Database System for ADP, which also was one of our concerns about enormous waste. And that Mr. Ates had been relieved of his duties.
There was no investigation.

In June 1991 I informed Gephardt that after the one meeting with Mr. Ates there had been no more meetings about our concerns of waste and theft. I reported the rejection of my Union Grievance which was to address the issues. *There was no investigation.*

I requested assistance from Gephardt's office in my filing a Whistleblower Complaint. *I received no assistance.*

In October 1991, instead of investigating my report for the House Agriculture committee, Gephardt's staff suggested that I mail my report directly to the committee. I did so, and I volunteered to testify for the committee at the hearings. My offers were not acknowledged nor investigated. Instead of working to solve the problem, the sub-committee issued a GAO report showing the problem.

"ADP MODERNIZATION Half-Billion Dollar FmHA Effort Lacks Adequate Planning and Oversight." *There was no investigation.*

I wrote Gephardt complaining that the committee did not use my evidence which clearly showed that the unjustified and unplanned purchase of the ORACLE database system will now waste another half-billion dollar ADP modernization effort. *There was no investigation.*

Fax on January 14, 1992, addressed to Gephardt,

ACCOUNTING CONTROLS, MISMANAGEMENT, AND WASTE IN GOVERNMENT—I have not received an answer from you, to my letter of December 23, 1991; therefore I again appeal to YOU, congressman, that my WHISTLE BLOWER COMPLAINT TO THE SPECIAL COUNSEL BE HEARD.

MILLIONS OF AMERICANS ARE ASKING, WHEN ARE YOU, IN CONGRESS GOING TO STOP CHAOTIC GOVERNMENT ACCOUNTING, AND ACCOUNT FOR TRILLIONS OF GOVERNMENT SPENDING, WASTE, AND FRAUD?
There was no investigation.

On September 9, 1992, by registered mail, I requested both President Bush and Congressman Gephardt to investigate my Whistleblower Complaint.

My enclosed WHISTLEBLOWER COMPLAINT Shows,

I. GROSS WASTE AND GROSS MISMANAGEMENT
Can congress, represented by Congressman Richard A. Gephardt, sit down, face to face with PRESIDENT George H.W. Bush, and lay out a plan to solve these serious problems of Computer Automation and INADEQUATE CONTROLS.
There was no answer nor investigation by either Bush nor Gephardt.

To Nancy Parker of Gephardt's office in Washington, on January 7, 1993, I Faxed six pages.

For the past two years, you and I have worked on the serious problem of federal MISMANAGEMENT of computer automation, which has serious government wide implications. President Clinton's new Secretary of Management and Budget, and the Secretary of Treasury will want to know about these serious problems, especially where INADEQUATE PROCESSING CONTROLS are causing CHAOTIC GOVERNMENT ACCOUNTING....When can you and your staff, meet with me and my advisors to review my report....We can meet either at Lemay Bank, at the CPA office, or a place of your choosing.

THERE WAS NO ANSWER, NO MEETING, *AND NO INVESTIGATION*

Throughout the next two years, I continued to write Gephardt, showing additional horror stories about computer hackers and computer waste. *There was no investigation.*

In July 1993, I received a letter from Gephardt, inviting me to join his Majority Leader's Club. His letter began,

> Dear Anthony,
> · I want you to join me in becoming a carpenter for our nation!
> Sam Rayburn, the powerful Texan and former Speaker of the
> House, used to say that any jackass can kick down a barn,
> but it takes a carpenter to build one.

I sent my check and became a Charter Member of the Majority Leader's Club, but there were no meetings of the Club nor with myself. Now this person wants to kick down Gephardt's barn!

Then after continuing appeals to Gephardt for a meeting to investigate my Whistleblower Complaint, on June 9, 1995, I received another denial as he concluded,

> ...I have reviewed my schedule for St. Louis, and unfortunately, my
> schedule does not permit an appointment in the near future."
> Regarding my Whistleblower Complaint, Gephardt suggested,
> ....there is a non-profit, non-partisan organization known as the
> Government Accountability Project (GAP) that may be interested in
> your concerns....I have enclosed some background information on
> GAP...." An enclosed GAP publication is titled,
> Courage Without Martyrdom, A Survival Guide for
> Whistleblowers.

There was *no investigation.*

Gephardt to Blame

I have conclusive evidence showing that Congressman Richard A. Gephardt acted irresponsibly by not stopping the computer waste of $500 million at the U. S. Department of Agriculture. And I have letters including reports written to Congressman Gephardt with copies sent to the U. S. General Accounting Office (GAO), which certainly prompted the GAO report titled, 'ADP MODERNIZATION Half-Billion Dollar FmHA Effort Lacks Adequate Planning and Oversight.'

Furthermore, Congressman Gephardt's misrepresentation and neglect of this serious matter has allowed continuing waste and fraud throughout government amounting to more than $50 billion of waste each year.

Undoubtedly computer technology companies have contributed to political campaigns, which is legal. But one must wonder if illegal gratuities were given to federal employees who by their unjustified purchasing of ineffective computer technology have created unreliable systems and controls, and have wasted billions of our tax dollars.

My conclusion is that when Congress does not represent its constituents, then government by the people is doomed to failure.

CHAPTER TEN
WORKING IN HELL

Working for the Autocratic Bureaucracy of government was like working in hell.

'You'd better shape up!'

While working at Agriculture, I found that most federal employees work long and hard to do the best job possible. That is, until they are beaten down and burned-out by the dictatorial whims of management.

I worked for Information Resources Management (IRM) with computer programming analysts who were responsible for designing, programming, and implementing individual computer automation job streams. Federal computer programmers showed me that they were among the best in the data processing industry. And they worked long and hard in futile efforts to fulfill the dreams of the Information Revolution.

Computer users, including financial management and program management, were dedicated, ambitious, and knew what they needed from computer automation and the information revolution. They also worked long and hard in their futile efforts to fulfill their dreams.

The Policy and Procedures branch of IRM was also diligent and worked long hours in futile efforts to fulfill these Information Revolution dreams. Unfortunately, Policy and Procedures personnel believe that User Design Requirements serve the same purpose as System Design Specifications as they did in the past. And they continue to schedule individual sub-system tasks without first having a plan or General Design about how the whole system will be built and fit together.

There was a total vacuum in the area of designing integrated computer systems. It appeared that every job given to the Programmer Analyst lacked forethought and planning. So much so that I thought I would lose my sanity. Fortunately, I had my personal work with electronics, patents, and designing electronic games as a diversity, which helped me to maintain a diligent work ethic.

I continued to do my assigned programming tasks in a professional manner. And I shared my extensive data processing experience with freely given and documented employee suggestions.

After ten years and the failure of five major computer automation efforts, I saw the frustration and burn-out of many fellow employees in all departments. Many dedicated and skilled employees left government, while others became complacent and are now waiting for retirement.

The harder I worked to perform my job in a professional manner, the more I was bypassed for promotions. And thanks to the American Federation of Federal Employees (AFGE), I was not fired.

While filing union grievances for non-promotion, the president of AFGE recognized a pattern of age discrimination. My class action discrimination suit languished in EEOC offices for about two years. Then it was kicked back to Agriculture for prompt individual reconciliation. After another year, I was offered a promotion with back pay, providing I retired in six months. When I protested that forced retirement was discriminatory, management changed the term "retired" to "resign." Fortunately with the Union's help, I received the promotion and did not resign.

Throughout my federal employment history, there was not one supervisor or manager who would talk with me about my suggestions and/or complaints about the tremendous waste of computer automation and information technology.

After months of communication with my congressman, I had one meeting with upper management. This newly hired manager agreed with many of my complaints and he took one of my immediate concerns to his boss. When the boss was questioned about this purchase of a $20 million computer database system without plans for its use, the manager was fired.

Agriculture's Assistant Secretary for Administration who oversaw the department's finances and IRM, was relieved of her duties after she asked too many questions about the department's $800 million ADP budget.

My numerous requests for investigation of computer waste by Agriculture's Office of Inspector General were ignored, until a meeting was ordered by Agriculture Secretary Mike Espy. After this one meeting, stories were leaked about the Secretary's conduct in office. Mr. Espy resigned. And there were no more meetings and no further investigation of computer waste.

My experience in government reminds me about Joe's story. In this story Joe died, was given a tour of heaven and hell, and was returned to earth for another chance. Joe told about the different places he had seen and he described one of the most interesting places of Hell. This hellish place was a large lake filled with brown smelly stuff. Each person was assigned to a 3 foot square area in the lake where that person needed to stand on tiptoes in order to breath. If you became tired, you would hold your nose, squat down, and rest awhile. After being rested or out of breath, you would return to your hellish tiptoe position. It did not look like a bad hell, until a devilish helper came to check on assigned positions. And before he could start up his motor boat, everybody yelled out in horror, "Don't make a wave."

While Windisch experienced "hell'" at the Department of Agriculture, other government departments are even worse off. For example, Comptroller John J. Hamre of the Pentagon cites "Astounding" accounting problems. He says, "It is pretty gummed up. I'll be long dead and gone before we ever reach nirvana when it comes to our accounting system."

Comptroller Hamre found:

- 450 accounting and management systems.
- 105 pieces of paper behind every military transaction.
- 40 percent of the department's checks still being signed by hand.
- An agency "up to its belt buckle" in computers but lacking integrated software.
- Military services each doing its own thing financially, with pay and personnel rolls so out of kilter that the Army recently kept paying more than two thousand people for months after they had left the ranks.

The Pentagon started to correct these findings and followed an ill-advised recommendation from GAO's 1992 "Financial Management Issues," to merge like financial systems. The Defense Finance and Accounting Services now provides Accounts Payable services for many different Pentagon agencies.

As a result of this mass production of Accounts Payable checks, manual paperwork was eliminated, including paperwork audit trails. A spot-audit in 1994 of nine contractors by the GAO uncovered one thousand mistakenly issued payments that were returned to the Defense Finance and Accounting Service. And during the first nine months of 1993, defense contractors returned $1.4 billion in overpayments to the Pentagon.

Senator John Glenn was quoted as saying, "Given the magnitude of waste in this small sample, I am concerned we are just looking at the tip of a very large iceberg."

AFGE Union Grievance

On June 10, 1991, I requested that the American Federation of Government Employees (AFGE) file the following Union Grievance. I hereby request that the AFGE Union file a grievance on behalf of Anthony J. Windisch, CDP, union member, against the ADP management of Farmers Home Administration, United States Department of Agriculture.

WHAT
Anthony J. Windisch. CDP, has been denied the potential for substantial earnings, because the management of Farmers Home Administration (FmHA) has not given due consideration to his more than two dozen Employee Suggestions submitted during the period of 1983 to the present.

This is in violation of the Agency's own published official instructions and administrative guidelines, and in violation of the Labor-Management Relations (LMR) Agreement between FmHA Finance Office and AFGE Local 3354.

BACKGROUND
Mr. Anthony J. Windisch, CDP, was hired by FmHA as a Computer Programmer Analyst, GS-334-11, in November, 1982. In December, 1983, Mr. Windisch applied for the position of Systems Accountant, GS-510-12, a position with responsibility for the design of Automated Data Processing (ADP) computer systems. Having a nationally recognized professional CDP certification, plus 10 years past experience as Manager of Computer Systems Design, Mr. Windisch believed he was more than qualified for this position of Systems Accountant.

His application was rejected, and also his documented qualifications appeal for FmHA certification to be recognized as being qualified for this position, was also rejected. Despite this official rejection for promotion into the position of computer systems design, in October 1984, Mr. Windisch was detailed to review the computer design aspects of the Accounting Program Delivery System (APDS), which was designed by Price Waterhouse. This responsibility was very similar to his previous position as Manager of Computer Systems Design! This assignment of monitoring APDS design lasted through the end of 1985.

After 1985, while working as a Computer Programmer Analyst, Mr. Windisch made numerous informal ADP design suggestions, and was told that 'Design'.was not part of his job nor responsibility. Because of this directive, Mr. Windisch was entitled to and did submit over two dozen Employee Suggestions involving the Design of ADP Systems.

By, 1987, Mr. Windisch became aware of the tremendous WASTE of computer resources at FmHA, and most alarming, was his discovery of the ABSENCE OF ADP FINANCIAL CONTROLS at FmHA. It was in 1987, that Mr. Windisch first submitted his Employee Suggestion to 'REORGANIZE ADP' so that the Accountants would be replaced by professional Computer Systems Analysts who would then be responsible for Work Analysis, Cost Justification, and finally, the Design of ADP SYSTEMS AND ADP CONTROLS.

This suggestion to REORGANIZE ADP was among seven (7) suggestions individually submitted by Mr. Windisch, from March 15 through June 15, 1987. On September 14, 1987 Mr. Windisch received a one page memo, announcing that six of these seven suggestions were rejected. These six suggestions were identified only by 6 unknown numbers, accompanied with a multiple choice set of generic reasons for the rejections.

Later, through a Dec. 3, 1987 memo, Mr. Windisch's missing 7th suggestion titled #78 without any other identification was accepted as a 'good idea.' After much research Mr. Windisch realized that this unknown #78 was his original suggestion 'To Guard Against Computer Hackers.'

In April, 1989, after reviewing the ROWE Report, Mr. Windisch sent a 'Response and Proposal' to the Assistant Administrator for Automated Information Services, FmHA, USDA, Mr. Mark A. Boster, wherein Mr. Windisch again proposed the Reorganization of ADP with additional data and referencing similar observations by the ROWE Report. In a July 17, 1989 letter to Mr. Windisch, Mr. Boster rejected Mr. Windisch's updated proposal because: I) Mr. Boster's draft organization package...should be forwarded to USDA for approval;' and 2) Mr. Windisch's proposal was 'too Drastic.'

In order to maintain a continuity with his 1987 suggestion, Mr. Windisch submitted Employee Suggestion FC-503 'REORGANIZE AIS' on 9/22/89 with over 100 pages of data updating prior documentation on the same subject. Without any discussion nor consultation with Mr. Windisch, suggestion FC-503 was rejected with a multi-page rebuttal dated Feb. 1, 1990, and signed by Clarence P. Squellati, Assistant Administrator, Finance Office.

In Mr. Windisch's considered professional judgement, the 1990 Reorganization of ADP did nothing to solve the problems of poorly designed ADP Systems, nor the ABSENCE OF ADP CONTROLS, so he submitted Employee Suggestion FC-523 to 'REORGANIZE AIS' on July 13, 1990 with additional documentation to substantiate that the same problems still existed. As of this date Mr. Windisch has received NO WRITTEN RESPONSE to Suggestion FC523.

DUE CONSIDERATION NOT GIVEN

A. RESPONSE OR NOT?
Mr. Boster's May 1, 1991 latest memo states:
'...we have responded to your employee suggestions.'

THE FACTS ARE:
1. There has been NO RESPONSE to Suggestion FC-523, which was submitted on July 13, 1990.

2. Although the 1987 Suggestion #78 'To Guard Against Computer Hackers' was accepted as a 'good idea,' on Dec. 3, 1987, there has been NO RESPONSE as to when or if it will be implemented.

Finance Office Procedure FL.300.7, page 8 states, 'V. TIME LIMITATIONS. 8. If the suggestion cannot be evaluated in 60 workdays, the ESC will notify the suggester to explain the reason for postponement and provide a revised evaluation completion date.'

B. ATTITUDE:
Management's attitude of Mr. Windisch's Employee Suggestions is reflected in their summary statement to FC-503,

'...it is evident Mr. Windisch routinely uses the suggestion program to interject his personal opinions and criticism over design and development decisions. Management and the Employee Suggestion Program should not encourage this attitude or behavior....'

A pamphlet entitled: 'FmHA Suggestion Program-Supervisor's Responsibility 'states '...Suggestions from Employees...must not be considered by Supervisors as criticisms of how things are being done.....'

C. RESPONSIBILITY:

1. Be receptive to employee suggestions: There is an atmosphere of resistance to Employees' suggestions.

2. Give Credit freely:
a) Although Mr. Windisch has received a letter of commendation from the Supervisor, Account Reconciliation Unit, for 'a superior job' in designing a 'State of The Art' Deposit Fund Online Reconciling Computer System, he has not received copies of this commendation.
b) Mr. Windisch was embarrassed when his ADP supervisor presented him with a pseudo award mocking his many suggestions.

3. Be appreciative of all ideas: Mr. Windisch was by-passed on 12 occasions for ADP promotion.
4. Help employees prepare suggestions: Supervisors refused to discuss suggestions with Mr. Windisch and would not help him prepare his suggestions, nor promote them, nor follow up to facilitate responses. In fact, because his supervisors frowned on any FmHA office preparation of his suggestions, Mr. Windisch was forced to prepare and type his suggestions at home.

5. Respect an employee's idea:
a) No respect for Mr. Windisch's CDP professional certification.
b) No respect for Mr. Windisch's 30 years of ADP experience as verified and reflected in the FC 503 rebuttal: 'The entire suggestion package consists mostly of the suggester's self-proclaimed credentials.'
6. Do not take participation in the Suggestion Program for granted. ADP Supervisors do not promote the Suggestion Program.
7. Encourage Suggestions and you will build employee enthusiasm. ADP Supervisors discourage suggestions.
8. Process suggestions promptly: ADP management does not process suggestions promptly.

REMEDY

That FmHA management reconsider and provide an objective review of each of the following four (4) Employee Suggestions:

1. Suggestion #78 'GUARD AGAINST COMPUTER HACKERS'
2. Suggestion FC-301 'PROVIDE BETTER AUDIT TRAIL'
3. Suggestion FC-523 'REORGANIZE AIS'
4. Suggestion FC-504 'DESIGN AND IMPLEMENT ALSIS'

This is to be done in accordance with the Employee Suggestion Program guidelines, and with the participation of a qualified ADP professional person from outside the Agency, plus Mr. Windisch, and his Union representative.

Management rejected grievance because:

A. Management gave prompt and proper consideration to all suggestions.
B. Management has the right to manage, and can decide not to implement even good suggestions.
C. LMR Agreement does not provide for an outsider to evaluate Employee Suggestions.

I submitted more than twenty-four Employee Suggestions which were all ignored and rejected by management. At a Christmas party, my supervisor read and presented an award certificate which read: 'TO Tony Windisch, THE MOST PROLIFIC EMPLOYEE AWARD FOR ALL THE WORK PUT INTO NUMEROUS EMPLOYEE SUGGESTIONS.'

Whistleblower Protection Act a Waste

The 1989 Whistleblower Protection Act separated the Office of Special Counsel (OSC) from the Merit Systems Protection Board (MSPB) and established OSC as an independent agency.

In 1991 I filed a Whistleblower Complaint about government waste and mismanagement of federal computer automation. My experience with the Office of Special Counsel (OSC) is reflected in a General Accounting Office (GAO) report.

The GAO, November 1993 report GAO/GGD-94-21 is titled, "Reasons for Whistleblower Complainants' Dissatisfaction needs to be Explored."

About 81 percent of the 662 respondents gave OSC a generally low to very low rating for overall effectiveness. OSC was consistently rated low for fairness, efficiency, competency, responsiveness, and communications.

Eight-five percent of complainants whose cases were closed by OSC's Complaints Examining Unit (CEU) rated OSC generally low to very low on overall effectiveness in handling their cases. Eighty-four percent believed they needed to obtain the services of a lawyer to protect their interests.

An explanation of the Complaint process is listed on pages one and two of the report:

"In order to successfully pursue a Whistleblower reprisal case, OSC said that it must develop sufficient evidence to show the following four elements exist:

- a protected disclosure was made by a covered federal employee;
- a personnel action was taken, not taken, or threatened after the protected disclosure;
- the employer had knowledge of the protected disclosure;
- a causal connection existed between the personnel action and the protected disclosure."

In my case, the opening statement of the OSC process is false. OSC did nothing to develop evidence for any of the four elements; and they gave me no instructions about procedures.

The odds are stacked against a complaint being investigated, because the inexperienced Complainant must prove all four elements. The Complaint Examining Unit (CEU) may decide that just one element is missing, and then it can reject and dismiss the case.

OSC closed my case and did not investigate because "...you have presented no evidence of gross mismanagement to substantiate your allegations."

Instead of investigating my evidence, OSC took the response from the guilty agency as proof that my protected disclosure was non-existent.

OSC also dismissed their primary responsibility by not requesting management to show just cause for my non-promotion to job positions for the "Design of Computer Systems" even though I have CDP certification of qualification from the Institute for Certification of Computer Professionals (ICCP), and had more than thirty years experience in managing, supervising, and designing computer automation systems.

Because my complaint involves a government-wide scandal of large proportions, I appealed several times to OSC for an investigation. Finally OSC said that they had no jurisdiction to investigate government waste. When I filed an appeal with the Merit Systems Protection Board (MSPB), they also said the MSPB had no jurisdiction to investigate government waste. I gave up this futile procedure to eliminate government waste.

In conjunction with my disclosure of waste, Assistant Deputy Administrator Edward Ates filed a Complaint with MSPB. He complained about being relieved of his duties after questioning his boss Mark Boster about computer waste. Mr. Ates won his case and was reinstated, but he found it best to resign and go to work for private business.

MSPB and OSC cannot give awards for punitive damage. There is no punitive action taken against offenders of the "Whistleblower Protection Act." And Mark Boster was allowed to continue his job, continuing to waste computer resources.

If the 'Whistleblower Protection Act' does not provide for investigation of mismanagement and waste, what is its purpose?

Whistleblower Act Still Dormant and Ineffective

On April 26, 1996 I sent a letter to Leon Panetta, the Advisor to President Clinton.

Dear Leon,
    RE: GOVERNMENT COMPUTERS ADD TO WASTE A FINANCIAL MANAGEMENT CRISIS
    PLEASE PERSUADE PRESIDENT CLINTON TO INVESTIGATE MY WHISTLE BLOWER COMPLAINT IN ORDER TO ADDRESS AND CORRECT A SERIOUS FINANCIAL MANAGEMENT CRISIS.
    Computer Czar Roger Johnson has left the General Services Administration without addressing this serious problem, per attached correspondence.

March 26, 1993 letter to Clinton - copy was sent to GSA.
August 12, 1993 letter received from GSA - no investigation.
February 13, 1996 letter sent to Roger Johnson of GSA.
February 27, 1996 follow-up letter to Roger Johnson.
On March 27, 1996 I learned that Roger Johnson had left
General Services Administration the first of March, '96."

A March 21, 1996 letter from GSA informed Windisch that Public Law 104-106 enacted in February 1996 had relieved GSA from all responsibility for the purchase of computers and information technology by government agencies.

On June 16, 1996 at 8:30 A.M. Windisch received a telephone call from Catherine McMullen of the Office of Special Counsel (OSC) informing him that the President's office had sent his Whistleblower video and other information to the OSC.

Windisch received an OSC disclosure form and a new Complaint number (OSC File No. MA-96-2193) on September 24, 1996.

After learning that the Complaint had reached the office of William E. Reukauf, Windisch sent a letter requesting status and procedures on November 13, 1996. "Please inform me of the following:
1. Has my complaint been accepted for processing?
2. Who has my Complaint?
3. What is the procedure for processing my Complaint?
4. What can I do to expedite processing?
5. What can Congressman Gephardt do to help?
6. What can Senator Ashcroft do to help?

WHISTLEBLOWER COMPLAINT DISCLOSURE (OSC File No. MA-92-1525) GROSS WASTE AND GROSS MISMANAGEMENT OF INFORMATION RESOURCES AND TECHNOLOGY, CAUSING UNRELIABLE SYSTEMS AND CONTROLS.

A. UNRELIABLE COMPUTER SYSTEMS ARE THE RESULT OF INADEQUATE PLANNING AND NO 'GENERAL DESIGN' FOR NEW SYSTEMS.

1. In 1984, an Information Resources Management (IRM) supervisor received national honors from the Association of Government Accountants (AGA) for adopting Life Cycle Methodology (LCM) procedures as a guide for the design and implementation of integrated computer systems.

a) A critical path scheduling chart for LCM procedures shows how Phase E "General Design" is most important, because here the basic system concept is born, as all subsystems are merged and integrated into one system.

2. Windisch discovered that LCM design procedures were not followed, and in 1987 he filed an Employee Suggestion to 'Reorganize Information Resources Management' whereby computer professionals are put in charge of designing and implementing integrated computer systems.

a) In 1989, Mark Boster responded to the complaint about non-performance of "General Design", and a new 1990 'Project Life Cycle' chart was issued which doesn't even show a procedure phase of "General Design."

3. In 1991 Windisch filed a 'Critical Report' with the House Agriculture committee complaining about the purchase of an ORACLE Database System without pre-planning and without a "General Design" for its use.

a) Windisch recommended 'Reorganize Information Resources Management' as a solution to the problem/s.

b) The Agriculture committee did not investigate the report, and did not accept Windisch's offer to testify.

c) Instead, the committee issued a General Accounting Office report titled, 'ADP MODERNIZATION Half-Billion Dollar FmHA Effort Lacks Adequate Planning and Oversight.'

4. Government-wide mismanagement of IRM is shown by a 1993 General Services Administration (GSA) book titled 'Information Resources Management Strategic Planning Guide.' This guide

65

illustrates planning to build a $500,000 house, but there is no hint of "General Design" planning for building integrated housing.

5. In 1994, Senator William Cohen reported, since 1990 the General Accounting Office published 74 reports about failures of information technology programs, consistently identifying problems with requirements analysis, program management, and cost/benefit analysis.

6. THE ABSENCE OF PRE-PLANNING AND "GENERAL DESIGN" CONTINUES.

B. UNRELIABLE COMPUTER CONTROLS RESULT FROM THE ABSENCE OF COMPUTER 'INTERNAL CONTROLS.'

1. At Agriculture, the General Ledger account for Loans Receivable cannot be balanced to the computer Program Loan Accounting System (PLAS) file, because there are no internal control totals on the computer PLAS file.

2. In 1985, while reviewing the 'Processing Controls' subsystem of the Accounting Program Delivery System (APDS), Anthony Windisch pointed to some serious control problems. And on 11/20/85 Jim Campbell said that Price Waterhouse was rewriting Program AOBR200 specifications and they were adding BALHEAD and BALDTL control records to the database as Mr. Windisch suggested. Unfortunately, this APDS system failed and was not implemented.

3. The Strategic Financial System Improvements (SFSI) project was initiated in 1986. Project 2-A-1 EVALUATE SYSTEM CONTROL IMPROVEMENTS included; Page 4-2.11 "...ensure that the database balances to the General Ledger..." and Page 4-2.13 "History to Database balancing requirements will be addressed as part of Project 4.A.1." Neither of these requirements was investigated and they were not implemented.

4. In 1987, Windisch submitted Employee Suggestion #78 'Guard Against Computer Hackers' which would establish 'Internal Control' totals on the computer PLAS loan file, and this PLAS database file would also be balanced to the computer Transaction History file. This suggestion was accepted as a good idea, but it was not investigated and it was not implemented.

5. The Office of Special Counsel (OSC) held no hearing/s nor investigation of my disclosure of missing 'Internal Controls,' Instead,

OSC showed their misunderstanding of the disclosure in an OSC letter dated August 27, 1992, 'You identified your disclosures as your suggestions over the years for improving the agency's security system for computer programs.'

6. THERE IS NO UNDERSTANDING OF THE MEANING NOR OF THE NEED FOR COMPUTER 'INTERNAL CONTROLS.'

C. THE SOLUTION FOR UNRELIABLE COMPUTER SYSTEMS AND CONTROLS IS 'REORGANIZE INFORMATION RESOURCES MANAGEMENT' WHEREBY COMPUTER PROFESSIONALS ARE PUT IN CHARGE OF DESIGNING AND IMPLEMENTING INTEGRATED COMPUTER SYSTEMS.

There has been no answer to this November 13 1996 letter, and telephone calls to Mr. Reukauf's office were not returned.

Can Whistleblowers Win?

Stories about Whistleblowers and their attorneys becoming millionaires are over-published and rare. It was attorney John Phillips who caused this limited success when he helped persuade Congress to strengthen little-known provisions of the False Claims Act, which was enacted during the Civil War to fight fraud against the Union Army.

The changes in the Act empowered taxpayers to sue unscrupulous contractors on their own in federal court. The government has the option of joining and managing the suit. If government doesn't get involved, a Whistleblower can obtain as much as 30 percent of any recovery. Attorney contingency fees range from 20 percent to 35 percent. This can be a win-win situation for the Whistleblower and attorney, because they have the government on their side.

The False Claims Act, is promoted by Taxpayers Against Fraud (TAF) which is a private, non-profit organization that exists to provide litigation assistance to private plaintiffs under the Act. In general the False Claims Act covers fraud involving any federally funded contract or program, with the exception of tax fraud. However the Act does not cover government waste and incompetence, no matter how many taxpayer dollars are being unnecessarily spent. TAF works solely with the False Claims Act. TAF has been accused of being in existence primarily to benefit its attorneys.

On the other hand, the Government Accountability Project (GAP) has a reputation for listening to all Whistleblowers from all areas of government and industry.

Each year GAP receives approximately one thousand requests for assistance, and gives free advice and guidance. But because of scarce funds, litigation assistance is limited.

On August 10, 1995, I received a letter from GAP, including the following story,

The Food Lion Corporation is the fastest growing grocery store chain in the United States and a notorious violator of consumer health and labor standards. Back in 1991, Food Lion employees began to report to GAP shocking abuses of food safety standards, such as grinding spoiled and expired meat into sausage, removing expiration dates from out-of-date products, washing off meat that is slimy, greenish and putrid, or soaking meat in bleach to conceal spoilage.

So acute was their fear, these employees offered the information only because of our vow to hold their identities in the strictest secrecy. In confidence, we took these employee concerns to the television network ABC, which after confirming these allegations, aired a national exposé on its investigative news show, *Primetime Live*, subjecting Lion Food to unprecedented levels of public scrutiny.

Food Lion's corporate attorneys could have advised the company to clean up its act, but instead they have decided to wage war against GAP. They have filed intrusive subpoenas against our staff, former legal clerk volunteers, and Board of Directors. If successful, this attack could torpedo our ability to promise confidentiality to anyone. In the meantime, all of us here are on the line both personally and professionally.

And there was a request for funds, "Please don't hesitate to send your gift of conscience right now. The need is immediate and great."

And it was reported that Food Lion filed suit against ABC *Primetime Live* for $2.5 billion in damages.

While blowing the whistle under the False Claims Act can be a win-win situation, blowing the whistle against government waste, appears to be a lose-lose game.

GAP's advice to obtain media publicity was also tried. More than a dozen TV shows were contacted. Most did not answer my correspondence, while others said that the problem was too big to fit into a thirty second sound bite. And still others said that the problem was too complex for the public to understand.

I also contacted the magazines and newspapers and got much the same story. My local newspaper said that they did not have enough people to investigate my story. And one assistant editor said that he did not find the story very interesting.

CHAPTER ELEVEN
CONCLUSION-CLASS ACTION SUIT

On May 6, 2008, I wrote to my United States Senator Claire McCaskill:

Dear Senator McCaskill,   RE: NATIONAL SECURITY CRISIS

I have not heard from you nor your Kansas City Regional Office since June 26, 2007, when I signed and returned the "PRIVACY ACT RELEASE FORM" to your Kansas City office.

Meanwhile, I have completed my 25 year work/study project, and on March 14, 2008, I reported to the public: "...CONGRESS IGNORES FEDERAL FINANCIAL AND COMPUTER MISMANAGEMENT INCLUDING POOR FINANCIAL AND POOR COMPUTER CONTROLS. CONGRESS ALSO AUTHORIZED "OPEN" COMPUTER SYSTEMS WITH INTERNET COMMUNICATIONS TO CREATE A PLAYGROUND FOR COMPUTER HACKERS...CONGRESS HAS CREATED A NATIONAL SECURITY CRISIS, THAT CAN DEVASTATE ALL OF US!..."

A. Please inform Congress by reading my enclosed text, "WHISTLEBLOWER REPORTS TO THE PUBLIC," while on the Senate floor and for the congressional record. (page 1 attached)

B. Have the Senate take corrective action by putting into law the (attached page 16) recommendations from my enclosed "DRAFT WHISITLEBLOWER CLASS-ACTION."

C. If you, as my Senator, do not have the authority to take corrective action, please ask President George W. Bush to use the power of his office to take corrective action.

I have recorded a detailed seminar on DVDs which documents and explains each phase of my Complaint.

Respectfully,
Anthony J. Windisch, CCP

Attached: 2 pages
Enclosed: booklet, "WHISTLEBLOWER REPORTS TO THE PUBLIC"
          booklet, "DRAFT WHISTLEBLOWER CLASS-ACTION"
          book, "GOVERNMENT COMPUTERS ADD TO WASTE"

<u>DRAFT</u> WHISTLEBLOWER CLASS-ACTION

Plaintiff in Pro Per

The _____ COURT OF _____ COUNTY

STATE _____

Anthony J. Windisch, Representative)
     CLASS ACTION   )
     Federal Whistleblowers   )
)
)
          Plaintiff   )
)
   V   )
)
Nancy Pelosi, Speaker of the)
U.S. House of Representatives)
and members of the House   )
)
         Defendants   )
	Case No. _____
	
	COMPLAINT

1. On July 16, 1987, Anthony J. Windisch filed an Employee Suggestion to "REORGANIZE COMPUTER MANAGEMENT" whereby computer professionals are hired to design and implement computer systems. The Suggestion was rejected. The General Accountability Office (GAO) investigated the Windisch complaint and reported to Congress about "COMPUTER MISMANAGEMENT" throughout the federal government. Congress has not addressed these problems and today there is a growing tangled mess of federal computer systems with "POOR COMPUTER SECURITY."

2. As a result of defendants' negligent behavior, GAO REPORTS, "...almost every federal agency has poor computer security...hostile nations or terrorists could use cyber-based tools and techniques to disrupt military operations, communications networks, and other information systems or networks..." The plaintiff's professional reputation was ruined, causing substantial pain and suffering, and lost income from his suggestion to REORGANIZE COMPUTER MANAGEMENT.

WHEREFORE, plaintiff prays for judgment against defendants in the sum of $2.5 billion ($2,500,000,000) plus costs and interest.

_____
Anthony J. Windisch, Plaintiff in Pro Per

CLASS–ACTION WHISTLEBLOWER COMPLAINT

COMPLAINT:

I, Anthony J. Windisch, seek accountability from Congress by filing a Class-Action Whistleblower Complaint on behalf of myself, and all federal Whistleblowers, against Nancy Pelosi, Speaker of the United States House of Representatives, and all other members of the House of Representatives.

1. Anthony J. Windisch has complained about financial Mismanagement, Computer Mismanagement, and Poor Computer Security at the U. S. Department of Agriculture.
2. The General Accountability Office (GAO) has:
   a. Investigated and confirmed the Windisch complaints.
   b. Informed Windisch and Congress that Financial Mismanagement, Computer Mismanagement and Poor Computer Security exists throughout the federal government.
3. **CONGRESS HAS NOT SHOWN ACCOUNTABILITY FOR FINANCIAL MISMANAGEMENT, COMPUTER MISMANAGEMENT AND POOR COMPUTER SECURITY WHICH HAS CAUSED A NATIONAL SECURITY CRISIS.**

PROBLEM:

Beginning with the 1980 Paperwork Reduction Act, the federal government continues with the **MISMANAGEMENT OF MAINFRAME COMPUTERS,** which has cost taxpayers **MORE THAN A TRILLION DOLLARS.** Mismanagement of Mainframe Computers has caused **FINANCIAL MISMANAGEMENT, POOR COMPUTER SECURITY** and continues to waste **MORE THAN FIFTY BILLION DOLLARS EACH YEAR.**

PREFACE:

The General Accountability Office (GAO) continues reporting to Congress about computer mismanagement, financial mismanagement, poor computer security, waste and fraud. But contrary to what most people believe, GAO has no authority to correct the problems that it reports. In addition, federal employees who blow the whistle on waste or fraud risk losing their jobs. And potential Whistleblowers are eliminated by giving their jobs to private contractors.

BACKGROUND:

Anthony J. Windisch is a certified computing professional (CCP), who documented his working for the federal government in his book titled, "GOVERNMENT COMPUTERS ADD TO WASTE - MASS CONSPIRACY TO DEFRAUD." His story is summarized in the attached article, "Government Computers Add To Waste."

71

Beginning in 1982, Anthony Windisch worked at the U.S. Department of Agriculture (USDA). He soon learned that the Systems Accountants, who were responsible for implementing 'State of the art' computer systems, did not understand the basic concepts of computer DATABASE design.

USDA converted a Burroughs computer operating system into an IBM computer operating system using Cullinet's Integrated Database Management System (IDMS).

With the new IBM computer operating system, because of an INCORRECT DATABASE DESIGN, the first night's processing of more than 100,000 daily FARM LOAN transactions ran for hours and hours, and was finally canceled because of computer DEVICE CONTENTION.

DEVICE CONTENTION occurred because of an INCORRECT DATABASE DESIGN. As a result, during the updating of LOAN transaction records onto four separate computer disk files, there was a constant random switching between the four computer Disk pack storage units, while updating only a few transactions at a time onto each computer Disk pack.

A CORRECT DATABASE DESIGN would allow continuous updating of loan transactions onto the first computer Disk storage file, then onto a second Disk storage file, then onto a third Disk storage file, and then onto a fourth Disk storage file.

Instead of correcting the INCORRECT DATABASE DESIGN, computer programmers decided to modify the Job Control Language (JCL). The original JCL was: 1. Sort the update records into logical report sequence. 2. Update the computer LOAN file in logical report sequence. 3. Print the update register report in logical report sequence.

A new JCL computer procedure was created: 1. Calculate and enter computer file location onto each LOAN transaction record. 2. Sort records into computer file location sequence. 3. Update the LOAN computer file in file location sequence. 4. Sort updated records into logical report sequence. 5. Print the update register report in logical report sequence.

After changing the job processing sequence for updating the computer LOAN file, the computer programmers realized that the LOAN "CONTROL TOTAL" amount records had been eliminated. And computer programmers decided that keeping a "CONTROL TOTAL" amount record was not necessary to meet their control requirements.

A few days later, the Assistant Administrator, Larry Miller, called an impromptu meeting with the computer programmers. He was disappointed with the poor use of the new Culprit "Report Writer." He said, "Congress was promised that 'upon request' farm LOAN reports would be produced within hours by using the new "Report Writer."

Windisch pointed out, "The new 'Report Writer' cannot be used on the LOAN computer Disk file because of "DEVICE CONTENTION." And Miller replied, "My supervisors have not made me aware of any problems. I will meet with you later."

After several meetings with Larry Miller, Windisch heard that Mr. Miller was fired, and there were no more meetings.

Years later, after the Loan Servicing Offices installed computers for online updating of the National mainframe computer LOAN file, Windisch wrote computer programs to provide on-line transaction history for viewing at the Servicing Offices. But a "Next-day Transaction register," which was required for update verification, could not be produced because of "DEVICE CONTENTION."

Without "Next-day Transaction Register" verification, GAO reported, "...(USDA) manages its loan portfolio manually by using color-coded index cards despite spending $200 million on computer systems to perform this task..."

Without maintaining a "CONTROL TOTAL" amount on the computer LOAN file, it was impossible to perform an agency DAILY AUDIT REQUIREMENT, and the balancing of the daily updating and TOTALS of the computer LOAN file to the TOTALS on the General ledger computer file was DISCONTINUED. Agency auditors were unaware that this AUDIT REQUIREMENT HAD BEEN DISCONTINUED.

TRY BALANCING YOUR CHECK BOOK WITHOUT KEEPING A "CONTROL TOTAL" AMOUNT FOR COMPARISON TO YOUR BANK STATEMENT AMOUNT.

Later, Windisch was assigned to rewrite the computer programs that produce Month End Loan reports. He complained to his supervisor, Pat Sinner, that the computer LOAN file did not include a "CONTROL TOTAL" amount on the computer LOAN file, and that without a "CONTROL TOTAL" amount for comparison, there was no way to verify that the TOTAL AMOUNT of loans on the new LOAN reports were correct.

After GAO wrongly accused Price Waterhouse for failing to complete the computer system design, Price Waterhouse closed their St. Louis government contracting office.

In 1990, Supervisor Patrick Sinner sent Windisch to a seminar where the Oracle Computer System was demonstrated. Windisch performed an independent feasibility study, which showed that IT WAS IMPOSSIBLE TO USE THE ORACLE COMPUTER SYSTEM AND PROVIDE **"USER REQUIREMENT SPECIFICATIONS"** such as **"COMPUTER SECURITY"** AND **"FINANCIAL CONTROLS"**, which was documented in the Accounting Program Delivery System (APDS).

Proposed online updating of the Oracle computer files would:
1. Eliminate the financial controls of nightly batch updating by the National Finance Office in St. Louis.
2. NOT eliminate the theft of loan payments and fraud such as erroneous 1% interest rates.
3. Eliminate use of the central Deposit Fund System which assures that each deposited loan payment is applied to a correct loan account.

Windisch also pointed out that the Oracle "OPEN" database system provides **"POOR COMPUTER SECURITY"**, and when connected with the mainframe computer, invites potential "hackers" to invade the mainframe computer.

Congressman Richard A. Gephardt prompted a meeting for Windisch with Assistant Administrator Edward Ates to review complaints about the Oracle database system. After the meeting with Windisch, when Edward Ates questioned his boss Mark Boster about the Oracle computer system and **"POOR COMPUTER SECURITY,"** Mark Boster fired Edward Ates.

In 1991, a story in GOVERNMENT COMPUTER NEWS questioned the motivation and integrity of the National Security Agency. **"Sharing Secrets** - Vendors of data base management systems are concerned about the way a data base security standard is being developed. The National Security Agency's National Computer Security Center (NCSC) has been working on its Trusted Database Interpretation for more than a year with the help of Oracle Corp., but the contract to help develop a draft standard was made public only recently.

The shroud of secrecy surrounding the data base standard naturally has fueled vendors' suspicions that Oracle has been unduly favored. The vendors have objected to the technological approach the draft standard adopts and to the competitive edge they believe Oracle has secured.

It is unclear how NCSC arrived at the decision to pick Oracle, though it has been suggested that Oracle submitted an unsolicited proposal. It also is unclear to whom the draft was sent for comment..."

GAO investigated Windisch's Complaint and sent report GAO/IMTEC-92-9 to the House Agriculture Committee, "ADP MODERNIZATION - Half-Billion Dollar FmHA Effort Lacks Adequate Planning and Oversight." This report shows the need to "Reorganize Computer Management," whereby computer professionals would be hired to design and implement 'state of the art' computer systems. This **GAO report also warned about "POOR COMPUTER SECURITY"**, "...While it is true that the government's open systems standards facilitate porting of software and interconnecting systems, they do not address design, procedural, or architectural incompatibility within an agency's application software or information systems..."

At GAO's suggestion, Windisch sent his "Critical Report" to the House Agriculture Committee, but Windisch was not allowed to testify.

In 1992, Leon Snead, Inspector General, USDA, wrote to Windisch and explained that POOR COMPUTER SECURITY was a government-wide problem. In 1987, Leon Snead participated in a President's Council on Integrity and Efficiency (PCIE).

Based on audits by the 10 agency inspector generals, the Council concluded, "...all of the agency computer systems reviewed had serious operating-system and software control deficiencies..." And "hackers" can "...access, modify and/or destroy an agency's computer data, programs and other resources without leaving an audit trail..."

Windisch tried to explain, that after **"ALL PHYSICAL CONTROL DEFICIENCIES"** discovered by PCIE are corrected, the use of an Oracle database system with its porting of computer software programs allows anyone to **"HACK"** into its interconnecting systems. But Leon Snead would not meet with Windisch.

In 1994, a federal "COMPUTER CHAOS" report, verified that Computer Mismanagement is a government-wide problem. This report cited Agriculture's wasteful Oracle Computer Project, "...after spending over $500 million modernizing its financial management systems, the effort was stopped before completion after management found out it did not really know what it was getting from its investment and the systems would not provide for effective oversight and fraud detection."

To answer Windisch's questions about Financial Mismanagement, GAO sent him report GAO/OCG-93-4TR titled, "FINANCIAL MANAGEMENT ISSUES...The Director of OMB (Office of Management and Budget) described the federal financial management system as "essentially a primitive cash budgeting system - without satisfactory controls or audits; without accruals; without balance sheets; without a clear picture of assets, liabilities, returns on investment, or risks."..."

"...Not only does the government do an abysmal job of rudimentary bookkeeping, but it is also far from having the modern financial systems one would expect of a superpower. At present, the federal government runs the world's largest financial operation without reliable information needed for making informed decisions. It annually spends about $1.5 trillion - almost a quarter of the country's gross national product - using unreliable systems and ineffective controls. And manages hundreds of programs, many of them individually larger than our nation's biggest publicly owned corporations, without adequate knowledge of their financial condition and the results they achieve..."

"...A growing consensus on the seriousness of the problems outlined above culminated in enactment of the Chief Financial Officers (CFO) Act in November 1990. This landmark law...represents the most far-reaching financial legislation in 40 years and provides an excellent blueprint for reform..."

Windisch questioned GAO's recommendation on page 29 of "Financial Management Issues," "...The government could also benefit from more cross-servicing, in which one agency provides financial services to another agency. Today, for instance, the Department of Agriculture provides payroll services to about 40 other agencies..." Windisch complained that this combining of financial computer processing for different agencies at one agency was contrary to the intent of the 1990 Chief Financial Officer (CFO) Act.

The GAO reply, "Unfortunately, we do not have many people in GAO who know a lot about computers."

Anthony Windisch wrote to President Bill Clinton in March, 1993, "...I claim that with INADEQUATE CONTROLS, IMPOSSIBLE AUDITS AND CHAOTIC ACCOUNTING, NOBODY KNOWS THE TRUE FINANCIAL CONDITION OF OUR COUNTRY. IF FOREIGN COUNTRIES ARE NOW CAUTIOUS ABOUT INVESTING IN OUR NATIONAL DEBT, WHAT WILL MY STORY DO TO THEIR CONFIDENCE?..." Instead of investigating the Windisch concerns about the commingling of agency funds, the U.S. Treasury Department formed the Financial Management Service (FMS).

On April 26, 1996, Windisch wrote to Presidential Advisor Leon Panetta, "PLEASE PERSUADE PRESIDENT CLINTON TO INVESTIGATE MY WHISTLE BLOWER COMPLAINT IN ORDER TO ADDRESS AND CORRECT A SERIOUS FINANCIAL MANAGEMENT CRISIS..." Windisch received a reply from the U.S. Office of Special Counsel, "This will acknowledge receipt of the above-referenced Complaint... (OSC File No. Ma-96-2193)." Then Presidential Advisor Leon Panetta resigned and Windisch's request for reconsideration of his Complaint was denied.

On June 1, 2000, Jack L. Brock, (GAO) Director, Governmentwide and Defense Information Systems, wrote, "Dear Mr. Windisch...Thank you for your recent letter regarding computer security. The need to strengthen computer security in both government and the private sector has been recognized ...I am enclosing a copy of my recent testimony before the U.S. Senate..."

Senate report GAO/T-AIMD-00-181, WARNING ABOUT "**POOR COMPUTER SECURITY**" IN THE GOVERNMENT, "...As noted in previous testimonies and reports, almost every federal agency has poor computer security. Federal agencies are not only at risk from computer virus attacks, but are also at serious risk of having their key systems and information assets compromised or damaged from both computer hackers, as well as unauthorized insiders...the potential for more catastrophic damage is significant...hostile nations or terrorists could use cyber-based tools and techniques to disrupt military operations, communications networks, and other information systems or networks..."

"**POOR COMPUTER SECURITY**" IN THE PRIVATE SECTOR, "...the worm/virus affected large corporations, such as AT&T, TWA, and Ford Motor Company; media outlets, such as the Washington Post, Dow Jones, ABC News; state governments; school systems; and credit unions, among many others...Inter-nationally, the virus affected businesses, organizations, and governments, including the International Monetary Fund, the British Parliament, Belgium's banking system, and companies in the Baltics, Denmark, Italy, Germany, Norway, the Netherlands, Sweden, and Switzerland..."

In 1995 it was reported, "During the Persian Gulf War a group of Dutch computer hackers offered Iraq their services to help snarl the Pentagon's electronic communications network. For mysterious reasons, Saddam Hussein turned them down. But a future foe might not, and could, thereby, gain success in penetrating America's military communications system."

Windisch was further alarmed when he read about terrorist Ziyad Sadaqa. "Authorities traced the satellite phone to Sadaqa, who had moved to Florida that year to take a job with Oracle, a computer software company..." The Oracle computer company would be a good place to learn "how to hack" into the federal computer files.

In 2002, Windisch wrote to President George W. Bush, and to Richard Clarke, Special Advisor for Cyberspace Security. "Iraq war planning must include the following strategic facts." The U.S. General Accounting Office (GAO) reported "...almost every federal agency has poor computer security... the potential for more catastrophic damage is significant... hostile nations or terrorists could use cyber-based tools and techniques to disrupt military operations, communication networks, and other information systems or networks..."

Richard Clarke was fired, and the Windisch concerns about a "NATIONAL SECURITY CRISIS" were not answered.

In 2002, Windisch wrote to Mr. Brock at GAO expressing serious concern about wide-spreading **"POOR COMPUTER SECURITY"** IN THE PRIVATE SECTOR. Windisch pointed out that federal inaction about the misuse of the Oracle computer system and **"POOR COMPUTER SECURITY"** IN THE GOVERNMENT, has given automatic approval to the Oracle Corp. implementation of a series of Financial Management Systems for use in THE PRIVATE SECTOR.

Shortly thereafter, Jack L. Brock, Director Government-wide and Defense Information Systems, was reassigned to be Managing Director, Acquisition and Sourcing Management.

November 1993, GAO/GGD-94-21 "WHISTLEBLOWER PROTECTION - Reasons for Whistleblower Complainants' Dissatisfaction Need To Be Explored." GAO surveyed 945 employees who sought protection from OSC (from 1989-1993) under the provisions of the 1989 Whistleblower Act, and received responses from 662.

"The results of our survey of those individuals (Windisch included) who sought whistleblower protection from OSC showed a general dissatisfaction with OSC and agency performance...

° About 81 percent of respondents gave OSC a generally low to very low rating for overall effectiveness...

° About 78 percent of respondents did not believe that OSC investigators obtained all of the information needed to investigate their claims.

° About 83 percent of respondents said they received a generally unfavorable to very unfavorable resolution of their complaints from OSC...

° About 88 percent of the respondents said that reprisals had actually taken place..."

While working at USDA, Windisch who is a certified computing professional (CCP), submitted a "REQUEST FOR CERTIFICATION OF BASIC ELIGIBILITY REQUIREMENTS FOR GS-510 ACCOUNTING SERIES GRADE-12 SYSTEMS ACCOUNTANT" with the responsibility for implementing 'state of the art' computer systems.

The "REQUEST" documented Windisch's 20 plus years of computer education and work experience, including being Manager of Computer Financial Systems at Wagner Electric Co.

On January 23, 1984, the Personnel Department replied "...Two supervisory accountants reviewed the information you provided...and determined that your'...background is insufficient to qualify (you) for the accounting series'."

In addition, after Windisch was bypassed for job promotions to Computer Programmer Analyst - Team Leader more than twenty times, the AFGE Union filed an Age Discrimination Complaint. And on February 1, 1988, Windisch wrote to the Assistant Administrator, Finance Office, USDA.

"...I am horrified by the harassment and new discrimination evidenced in your two documents of Jan. 14 and Jan. 22, 1988.

...In the first instance you "offer" to rob me of my individual rights to retirement options which I have earned! Are not mine and others' rights protected by the federal law?

Then in the second instance, rather than reconciling my registered complaints as they effect my employment position, you simply demand a forced resignation...eliminating my employment position!

Your repeated demands make me fearful that you intend to terminate my employment one way or another, with or without settlement of this matter! These instances of new progressive harassment highlight the on-going age discrimination!

You concluded each correspondence with the assurance "it is further understood and agreed that the complainant is to be free of any reprisal in connection with the subject matter."

Congressman Richard A. Gephardt wrote to Windisch, "This will acknowledge receipt of your recent letter regarding your whistleblower complaint from many years ago. As you know, you contacted the appropriate agencies and committees regarding this matter some time ago. There is no action I can take to investigate or assist you with this issue. Since you are dissatisfied with the Office of the Special Counsel's handling of this matter, I can only reiterate that you seek legal counsel for advice regarding any recourse that might be available."

After receiving the Gephardt rejection letter, Congressman James Talent offered to investigate Windisch's Complaint. A short time later Talent's office informed Windisch that Talent would not investigate the Complaint because of an unwritten rule of legislative courtesy where "A congressman may not investigate a Complaint outside their own jurisdiction."

In 2000, Windisch ran for congress on the Reform Party ticket. He participated in the Palm Beach Reform Party National Convention, but the news media seemed to ignore him and would not publish his issues.

In 1997, as the Senate and House Banking committees were working on a new Banking Reform bill, Federal Reserve Chairman Alan Greenspan warned about the commingling of federally insured bank deposits with Wall Street trading. "...the lines between banks, financial institutions and commercial firms are rapidly blurring, boosting the need for regulatory oversight...it's pretty apparent that the dividing line which segregates commerce and finance and finance and banking will continuously erode as the (computer) technology increases..."

Windisch wrote to President Bill Clinton, and the Treasury Department replied on August 24, 1998. "Dear Mr. Windisch...Thank you for the letter and accompanying information you sent to President Clinton concerning the banking reform bill, government financial management, and recent financial institution mergers..."

"Your letter (and accompanying information) also raises concerns that many consumers have with recent mergers in the financial services industry. Because of your interest in this subject, I am enclosing recent Treasury Department testimony on issues raised by large-scale financial institution mergers..."

Treasury report RR-2405 to the House Banking and Financial Services Committee, on page 5, "Some have raised concerns that larger and larger mergers may create institutions that would be considered "too big to fail" if they were threatened with insolvency, increasing pressure on the government to protect uninsured depositors and other creditors from loss in order to avoid systemic risk."

"...Systemic risk refers to the possibility of a sudden, usually unexpected event disrupting the financial markets quickly enough and on a large enough scale to cause significant harm to the real economy..."

"...<u>Cascades</u>. Systemic risk may arise from the business that banks and other financial institutions conduct with each other, e.g. small banks typically hold deposits in larger banks. The failure of a large bank or other financial firm could trigger in domino-like fashion the failures of other firms to which it owes money. The fear of a cascade of losses was a major reason why the Government extended protection to all depositors of the failed Continental Illinois Bank in 1984..."

As a result of Banking Reform, Citigroup Inc. became the world's largest financial-services company. It was reported that Citigroup "...was embroiled in a series of scrapes that hurt its reputation...is selling off some operations, such as asset-management and life-insurance units...It lost its private-banking license in Japan...faced probes of an aggressive bond-trading strategy in London...drew flack over its role in financing fraud-ridden companies including Enron Corp., Worldcom Inc., Adelphia Communications and Parmalat... faced billions of dollars in fines and settlements...etc..."

In 2003, Windisch again requested help from the Office of Special Counsel (OSC) regarding his Complaint about Federal Computer Mismanagement, Financial Mismanagement, and Poor Computer Security.

Windisch received several pamphlets from the OSC. A general pamphlet describes, "THE ROLE OF THE U.S. OFFICE OF SPECIAL COUNSEL... ° Protecting Federal Whistleblowers ° Investigating and Prosecuting Prohibited Personnel Practices... The U.S. Office of Special Counsel (OSC) is an independent federal investigative and prosecutorial agency..."

A second pamphlet, Form OSC-12 (2/02), explains, "...OSC does **NOT** have authority to investigate the disclosures that it receives. The law provides the OSC will (a) refer protected disclosures that establish a substantial likelihood of wrongdoing to the appropriate agency head, and (b) require the agency head to conduct an investigation, and submit a written report on the findings of the investigation to the Special Counsel." (emphasis of **NOT** is in the original text)

Pamphlet OSC-11 (2-02) explains, "OSC has no jurisdiction over employees of: ° the Central Intelligence Agency; ° the National Security Agency; ° the General Accounting (Accountability) Office; ° the Federal Bureau of Investi-gation; ° the Federal Aviation Administration; ° the U.S. Postal Service; ° other intelligence agencies excluded from coverage by the President;..."

In 2005, Windisch wrote a series of letters to the U.S. Justice Department requesting an investigation "of my Complaint about Computer Mismanagement and Financial Mismanagement which has caused a NATIONAL SECURITY CRISIS..." All requests for an investigation by the Justice Department were denied.

On the other hand, a ST. LOUIS POST-DISPATCH, PARADE article on September 9, 2001 titled "She Seeks Justice" describes how the Justice Department has spent more than $31 million dollars defending Computer Mismanagement and Financial Mismanagement at the U.S. Interior Department.

During this Blackfeet Indians class-action litigation, "...The presiding federal district judge, Royce Lamberth, twice ordered Interior and Treasury to produce documents involving the Individual Indian Money trust fund. Despite promises to do so, a special investigator appointed by Judge Lamberth discovered that during the course of the proceedings, Interior had in fact been destroying documents. What's more, Treasury officials had shredded 162 cartons of ledgers listing transactions and disbursements plus records of uncashed checks - some 100 years old - that never reached their intended Indian recipients..."

Later it was reported, "...In an extraordinary step approved by a federal judge (Lamberth), a computer expert hacked his way into a government-run Denver-based financial system this summer, created a false account and later altered yet another account. All this happened without the hacker being detected..." Review Jim Lehrer NEWS HOUR video.

THIS INTERIOR DEPARTMENT STORY IS CLEAR HORRIFYING PROOF OF WHAT IS HAPPENING <u>THROUGHOUT</u> THE FEDERAL GOVERNMENT.

On November 2, 2005, Windisch wrote to "The Honorable John Warner, Chairman, Committee on Armed Services...
Dear Chairman,

RE: NATIONAL SECURITY CRISIS
Please read my attached three page story showing how and why we have a National Security Crisis.

WHAT WILL YOUR ARMED SERVICES COMMITTEE DO TO ADDRESS THIS NATIONAL SECURITY CRISIS?..."

Senator Warner answered Windisch on November 21, 2005. "Dear Mr. Windisch: Thank you for contacting me regarding your request for assistance...Senatorial courtesy, a long-standing tradition in the United States Senate, dictates that a Senator be given the opportunity to assist the constituents they were elected to represent. Therefore, as a matter of courtesy, I am forwarding your correspondence to the Honorable Christopher Bond who represents the State of Missouri so that he can follow up with your case..."

On the other hand, when Windisch has written on his own to Senator Bond and other representatives, he was told that his representatives can make sure that his request for assistance is sent to the appropriate committee, but they had no control over how the committee (such as the Warner Armed Services committee) handles his request.

Meanwhile, there are continuing problems at USDA. January 2004, GAO-04-154, "INFORMATION SECURITY - Further Efforts Needed to Address Serious Weaknesses at USDA... Significant, pervasive information security control weaknesses exist..."

AND ALTHOUGH "...Significant, pervasive information security control weaknesses exist...", USDA IS CLOSING 800 OF ITS 2400 SERVICING OFFICES BECAUSE OF THE VOLUME OF INFORMATION THAT IS AVAILABLE FROM "OPEN" ORACLE COMPUTER SYSTEMS.

And governmentwide COMPUTER MISMANAGEMENT continues. Report GAO-04-615, "DOD BUSINESS SYSTEMS MODERNIZATION - Billions Continue to be invested with Inadequate Management oversight and Accountability...The Defense Department's Information Technology (IT) management blunders have also adversely affected U.S. military units and service members, including those fighting in Iraq and Afghanistan."

August 2006, report GAO-06-659, "INFORMATION SECURITY - Federal Reserve Needs to Address Treasury Auction Systems" The General Accountability Office (GAO) concludes, "...In general, the FRBs (Federal Reserve Banks) had implemented effective information system controls over the mainframe (computer) applications...On the distributed-based systems and supporting network environment used for Treasury auctions, however, they had not fully implemented information system controls to protect the confidentiality, integrity, and availability of sensitive and financial information..."

The FRBs misuse of "OPEN" computer database systems for its distributed-based systems shows how there is continuing "POOR COMPUTER SECURITY" throughout the federal government.

Report GAO-002-317, "FINANCIAL MANAGEMENT SERVICE - Significant Weaknesses in Computer Controls Continue...The pervasiveness of the computer control weaknesses - both old and new - at FMS (Financial Management Service) and its contractor data centers place billions of dollars of payments and collections at risk of loss or fraud..."

AGAIN, this GAO report warns about the increasing problems of **"POOR COMPUTER SECURITY,"** "...The severity of these risks magnifies as FMS expands its networked environment through the migration of its financial applications from mainframes to client-server environments..."

IN GAO-002-317, IN UNSEEMLY JEST, GAO REPORTS THAT THE TREASURY DEPARTMENT'S FMS IS "...the government's financial manager, central disburser, and collections agency as well as its accountant and reporter of financial information..."

ANTHONY WINDISCH COMPLAINS THAT THE UNITED STATES TREASURY DEPARTMENT OPERATES ITS FINANCIAL MANAGEMENT SERVICE (FMS) ILLEGALLY AND CONTRARY TO THE 1990 CHIEF FINANCIAL OFFICER (CFO) ACT. BECAUSE THE CFO ACT DICTATES THAT THE CHIEF FINANCIAL OFFICER FROM EACH AGENCY MUST BE HELD ACCOUNTABLE FOR ALL FINANCIAL REPORTING ABOUT THEIR AGENCY.

All Americans must read the attached article, "Government loses track of its money." This is a story about the General Accountability Office (GAO) audit of Federal Consolidated Financial Statements, which the GAO declared to be an **"UNMITIGATED DISASTER."** (emphasis added)

Congress has shown "NO ACCOUNTABILITY" for this DISASTROUS AUDIT, while THE U. S. TREASURY DEPARTMENT AND ITS FINANCIAL MANAGEMENT SERVICE (FMS) CONTINUE TO OPERATE A FINANCIAL MANAGEMENT SYSTEM THAT IS "...essentially a primitive cash budgeting system - without satisfactory controls or audits; without accruals; without balance sheets; without a clear picture of assets, liabilities, returns on investments, or risks..."

In addition, CONGRESS HAS SHOWN "NO ACCOUNTABILITY" FOR CONTINUING GAO REPORTS CONCERNING COMPUTER MISMANAGEMENT AND POOR COMPUTER SECURITY, WHICH HAS CAUSED A **"NATIONAL SECURITY CRISIS."**

CONGRESS MUST BE HELD ACCOUNTABLE FOR OUR NATIONAL SECURITY CRISIS.

A. CONGRESS MUST ADDRESS OUR "NATIONAL SECURITY CRISIS" BY CORRECTING "POOR COMPUTER SECURITY." AND IN CONJUNCTION, CONGRESS MUST "REORGANIZE COMPUTER MANAGEMENT," WHEREBY CERTIFIED COMPUTER PROFESSIONALS ARE HIRED TO DESIGN AND IMPLEMENT 'STATE OF THE ART' COMPUTER SYSTEMS,

B. CONGRESS MUST OUTLAW THE TREASURY DEPARTMENT'S FMS, AND ITS "...primitive cash budgeting system..."

C. CONGRESS MUST REINFORCE THE "CHIEF FINANCIAL OFFICER ACT," AND GIVE A TRUTHFUL FINANCIAL ACCOUNTING TO THE AMERICAN PEOPLE.

D. CONGRESS MUST REWRITE THE "WHISTLEBLOWER PROTECTION ACT" (WPA), WHEREBY WPA's "OFFICE OF SPECIAL COUNSEL" (OSC) IS A DEPARTMENT WITHIN THE GENERAL ACCOUNTABILITY OFFICE (GAO), AND GIVES GAO THE AUTHORITY AND RESPONSIBILITY TO:
1. PROSECUTE WRONGDOERS, AND
2. OFFER SOLUTIONS FOR PROBLEMS OF WASTE AND FRAUD.

Windisch claims that MISMANAGEMENT OF MAINFRAME COMPUTERS, FINANCIAL MISMANAGEMENT AND POOR COMPUTER SECURITY continues to **WASTE MORE THAN FIFTY BILLION DOLLARS EACH YEAR.**

Windisch seeks an award for his Employee Suggestion to "REORGANIZE COMPUTER MANAGEMENT" of 5 percent times $500 billion in savings equal to $2.5 billion.

Award will be distributed as follows:
1. Sixty percent to 1,000 federal whistleblowers surveyed for report GAO/GGD-94-21, and others named by Windisch.
2. Twenty percent to attorneys who work based on contingency.
3. Twenty percent to Anthony Windisch, his consultants and constituents.

Respectfully,
Anthony J. Windisch, CCP

85